PLAIN TALK ON
Timothy, Titus and Philemon

BOOKS BY DR. GUTZKE . . .

Plain Talk About Christian Words
Plain Talk on Genesis
Plain Talk on Exodus
Plain Talk on Isaiah
Plain Talk on Matthew
Plain Talk on Mark
Plain Talk on Luke
Plain Talk on John
Plain Talk on Acts
Plain Talk on Romans
Plain Talk on First and Second Corinthians
Plain Talk on Galatians
Plain Talk on Ephesians
Plain Talk on Philippians
Plain Talk on Timothy, Titus and Philemon
Plain Talk on Hebrews
Plain Talk on James
Plain Talk on the Epistles of John

PLAIN TALK ON Timothy, Titus and Philemon

MANFORD GEORGE GUTZKE
PH. D.

zondervan
publishing house

PLAIN TALK ON TIMOTHY, TITUS AND PHILEMON
© 1978 by Manford George Gutzke
Grand Rapids, Michigan

Library of Congress Cataloging in Publication Data

Gutzke, Manford George.
   Plain talk on Timothy, Titus and Philemon.
    1. Bible. N.T. Pastoral epistles—Commentaries.
    2. Bible. N.T. Philemon—Commentaries. I. Title.
BS2735.3.G86   227'.83'06   78-11065
ISBN 0-310-25661-5

All rights reserved. No part of this publication may be reproduced, stored in a retrieval system, or transmitted in any form or by any means, electronic, mechanical, photocopy, recording, or otherwise, without the prior permission of the publisher.

Printed in the United States of America.

CONTENTS

First Timothy

1. Timothy's Assignment 11
2. The Purpose of the Gospel 14
3. The Lord's Part in Salvation 18
4. Paul Was a Pattern 22
5. The Importance of a Good Conscience 25
6. Prayer for Public Officials 28
7. One Mediator 31
8. Paul's Basic Emphasis 34
9. Proper Dress for a Woman 38
10. The Status of Woman 41
11. The Pattern of a Good Elder 45
12. The Importance of a Good Reputation 49
13. Requirements for a Deacon 52
14. More About Deacons 55
15. The Mystery of Godliness 58
16. Some Doctrines Should Be Rejected 61
17. Good Doctrine Should Be Preached 64
18. Godliness Is Very Important 67
19. The Minister of the Gospel Should Be an Example   71
20. The Minister Is Responsible 75
21. Practical Guidance For Godly Conduct 79
22. Honest Responsibility Is Essential 82
23. The Unworthy Should Not Receive Charity Benefits   85
24. Treatment of Other Believers Should Be Godly ... 88
25. The Minister Must Judge Faithfully 91
26. The Gospel Accepts the Social Order As It Is 94
27. Striving to Be Rich Is Dangerous 97
28. Paul's Advice to Timothy 100
29. How Should the Rich Be Cautious? 103
30. The Danger in Science 106

Second Timothy

1. Paul's Greeting to Timothy 111
2. Paul's Admonition to Timothy 115
3. Paul's Sustaining Confidence 119
4. Paul's Further Advice to Timothy 123
5. Paul Appreciated Personal Support 127

6. Paul Urges Timothy to Be a Good Soldier 130
7. The Preacher Must Practice What He Preaches ... 134
8. The Issue of the Gospel Is Simple 137
9. Paul's Advice to Believers 140
10. The Faithful Witness Must Be Careful in His Conduct 144
11. Sin Will Grow Worse and Worse 148
12. The Weakness of Pretense 151
13. Opponents of the Gospel 154
14. Timothy's Fortunate Childhood 158
15. The Inspiration of Scripture 161
16. Paul's Advice to Timothy 165
17. The Confidence of a Good Conscience 169
18. Paul's Fellow Workers 173
19. Paul's Deliverance in the Roman Court 177
20. Personal Greeting 181

Titus

1. The Eternal Gospel........................... 187
2. Leaders Should Be Good Examples 190
3. False Leaders Should Be Sharply Rebuked 193
4. Evil Conduct Is Mark of Wrong Doctrine........ 196
5. Admonitions to the Mature 199
6. Admonitions to the Young and to Servants 201
7. The Function of Grace 204
8. Paul Was an Example......................... 207
9. Believers Should Maintain Good Works 209
10. Believers Are Special Persons.................. 212

Philemon

1. Paul Thanked God for Philemon................ 219
2. Philemon Was Helpful to Other Believers 223
3. Philemon Was Asked to Receive Onesimus Graciously...................................... 227
4. Paul Asked Philemon for a Personal Favor 230
5. Paul's Confidence in Philemon 233

First Timothy

Chapter 1

TIMOTHY'S ASSIGNMENT

Can you understand how, when a beloved friend has an important position, you might want to offer him help to do the best possible job?

> Paul, an apostle of Jesus Christ by the commandment of God our Saviour, and Lord Jesus Christ, which is our hope; unto Timothy, my own son in the faith: Grace, mercy, and peace, from God our Father and Jesus Christ our Lord. As I besought thee to abide still at Ephesus, when I went into Macedonia, that thou mightest charge some that they teach no other doctrine, neither give heed to fables and endless genealogies, which minister questions, rather than godly edifying which is in faith: so do (1 Tim. 1:1-4).

Our study concerns the correspondence between Paul and Timothy, an older person writing to a younger person. More than that, an older preacher is writing to a younger preacher. What can an older person be expected to contribute to a younger person? There is his experience, and in a real sense there is no substitute for experience. After all, Paul could tell this young man what would be before him. Telling someone anything about his work is always a ticklish proposition, especially telling a young person about his work; because most young people have the idea that they can do a better job than has ever been done before.

The younger generation feels it is going forward. This is the way the average young person is inclined to look forward into the future: "I have not been there, but I am really going to do it right." The older person who has been there, and who knows what the situation is, will do his best to give the young person all the help he can as he goes along. Paul started out the letter to Timothy by identifying himself. He did not say anything about his experience. He did not say anything about what he had learned and how much had happened to him. He brought to Timothy's mind that he, Paul, was a man sent from the Lord and authorized by the Lord to declare His Gospel. He was trusted by the Lord with preaching. It is from the standpoint of an apostle of Jesus Christ, a responsible representative of the Lord Jesus Christ, that this older man writes to the younger man.

Paul's attitude toward Timothy was one of affection. Paul really appreciated the young man. When Paul talked about Timothy in writing to the Philippians he said:

> For I have no man likeminded, who will naturally care for your state (Phil. 2:20).

Paul began his message with these words: "Grace, mercy, and peace, from God our Father and Jesus Christ our Lord." This was much more than just so many words of greeting. This included both prayer and benediction. Grace was what the old apostle wanted the young minister to have. Grace applies primarily to the weakness of men. It is what man needs and does not have, but what God will give him. Grace is not only God's mercy in pardoning the believer, but it is also God's provision that he may be strengthened. It is the grace of God in the heart that enables a person to think right and to do right.

Timothy was a human being, and a sensitive person. He would have known in his own conscience the things that had not been right in his life. He would feel that in his own strength he would be disqualified as a minister. So Paul prayed that mercy might be extended to this young man, and also peace. Peace has reference to contact with this world. It is the world that upsets us. Things press in on us. The uncertainty of the future disturbs us. The memory of many things in the past haunts us. Paul prayed for Timothy to have peace.

> As I besought thee to abide still at Ephesus, when I went into Macedonia, that thou mightest charge some that they teach no other doctrine, neither give heed to fables and endless genealogies, which minister questions, rather than godly edifying which is in faith: so do (1 Tim. 1:3-4).

This long statement indicates what Paul had in mind when he gave Timothy the assignment to minister in Ephesus. When we look at it closely, we can see what Timothy was to do at

Ephesus. He was to assume responsibility to see that what was being preached and taught was the right thing.

By the way, what do you think about the tendency today for people to suggest that everybody should have equal time? Do you think that is sound? Do you think that if you have a certain amount of clean elements to go into your food, you should also allow a certain amount of dirty elements to go into the food? Give all kinds equal time! Do you believe in it? If you take certain precautions to make sure that you are healthy and well, should you also give equal opportunity for microbes of diseases to get into you? Why should you be so exclusive and shut out all the destructive things in order that you could live? Does that make sense? Perhaps you will think I am writing foolishly. But how foolish can people be? Let us ask again about this popular mood that anybody is to be free to do anything he wants to do with no specific guidance.

That view is not approved in the Bible. God is concerned, and God is righteous. He stands straight up and down. He hates evil, and He does not allow equal time for any part of it. He is against it. If I am going to stand with Him, I must assume responsibility to stand up for that which is right and to stand up against that which is wrong. Here is Paul telling this young man, "I am leaving you over there at Ephesus to make sure that those people are careful about what they teach." Note the specific guidance that was offered: "You have the message; see to it that it is preached."

"Neither give heed to fables and endless genealogies." Fables are stories. People make up fictional ideas and then talk about them just because they sound impressive. Some people start reading in Matthew and get hung up in the genealogies of the first chapter. By the time they finish talking about that, it is time to go home. Spending time on discussing dark spots in Scripture will waste all the time you have. When all is said and done in such discussion, you have more questions than you had when you started. None of that sort of discussion will contribute to faith. So Paul tells this young man, "I have left you there with responsibility to oversee the situation. Do what you can to edify the believers, because preaching and teaching should never be the source of confusion and controversy."

Chapter 2

THE PURPOSE OF THE GOSPEL

Could you say in one sentence what the Gospel of Jesus Christ will do for any willing believer?

> Now the end of the commandment is charity out of a pure heart, and of a good conscience, and of faith unfeigned: from which some having swerved have turned aside unto vain jangling; desiring to be teachers of the law; understanding neither what they say, nor whereof they affirm. But we know that the law is good, if a man use it lawfully; knowing this, that the law is not made for a righteous man, but for the lawless and disobedient, for the ungodly and for sinners, for unholy and profane, for murderers of fathers and murderers of mothers, for manslayers, for whoremongers, for them that defile themselves with mankind, for menstealers, for liars, for perjured persons, and if there be any other thing that is contrary to sound doctrine; according to the glorious gospel of the blessed God, which was committed to my trust (1 Tim. 1:5-11).

Why should I become a believer? What difference would it really make? Or, to put it another way, if I become a believer in Jesus Christ, will it make any difference in me? Many who hear the preaching of the Gospel miss the boat. I remember once when I was living in Winnipeg in Manitoba, Canada, I was waiting to catch a train. I was early at the depot, so I bought myself a paper and began to read. I had bought my ticket, had it in my pocket, and was sitting there reading. I read until thirty minutes after the train was gone. That day I learned what it feels like to walk twenty-seven miles. Now remember, I had my ticket. I was in the right place. I wanted to go, but I missed the train.

I know that becoming a believer is based on something very simple. It is as simple as my sin, my inward inclination, in

The Purpose of the Gospel

which I do not want the things of God. Without help I could not have turned to Him nor believed in Him. Without His help I would never have committed myself to Him. But God was gracious. He sent His Son to die for my sins, to carry them away; and He gave His Holy Spirit into my heart so that I could have His presence with me. He surrounded me with witnesses to encourage me. God has been saving me in Christ Jesus in a wonderful way.

Everything that I have said so far is actually for you, and right here a big mistake can be made. A person may know all I have said and yet not do anything about it. Remember, I had my ticket. I had paid my fare. I wanted to go; I was willing to go. But I did not get on the train. To believe is to get on the train. Believing has an element of obedience to the will of God. When you yield to Him, certain results will follow.

As Paul was writing to Timothy, this was the way he put it:

> Now the end of the commandment is charity out of a pure heart, and of a good conscience, and of faith unfeigned (1 Tim. 1:5).

You might say the purpose, the end of the commandment, the goal towards which we move, is charity out of a pure heart. We can understand it better if we use the word "love" for "charity." Then we can put in the word "purified," and that will help. Thus we see the result is love from a purified heart, a sincere heart, when the inward consciousness is not blurred or marred or blemished by any selfishness. This does not so much mean love *and* a good conscience as it means love *out* of a good conscience. By a good conscience, we understand that the believer sincerely, conscientiously responds to the situations of living in the way he inwardly feels that he ought.

The word "unfeigned" means unpretended, genuine, real. This brings to my mind a kind of warning. Faith is something that can be pretended. How would you pretend it? You could say you have it when you do not. Who would know? Who is going to look into your heart? We can be reminded of the words of the Lord Jesus Christ who said, "By their fruits ye shall know them." So this is the end of the commandment. But by way of contrast Paul goes on to point out to Timothy,

> From which some having swerved have turned aside unto vain jangling (1 Tim. 1:6).

Some have lost their way, and have missed the mark. They have turned aside into vain talking.

> Desiring to be teachers of the law; understanding neither what they say, nor whereof they affirm (1 Tim. 1:7).

This reminds us that many people argue religion who do not have any. As I was going over this in my mind, I realized something that I need always to remember. Paul did not argue about how he knew this. He did not give any reasons for his judgment. He simply put it that way. He said himself there were people who offered to explain passages of Scripture, although they did not understand what they were talking about. Even today we hear people who never read the Bible talking about it. We hear people who never pray discussing whether or not God will answer prayer. Now Paul would say all such kind of discussion is vain.

Then he goes on to say something very definite about the Scripture:

> But we know that the law is good, if a man use it lawfully (1 Tim. 1:8).

There is nothing wrong about the law. There are people who in interpreting Scripture will say that we are free from the law. This statement could be very idle and very misleading. When Paul writes, "The law is good, if a man use it lawfully," he means that if it is used for its intended purpose it will be beneficial.

> Knowing this, that the law is not made for a righteous man, but for the lawless and disobedient, for the ungodly and for sinners, for unholy and profane, for murderers of fathers and murderers of mothers, for manslayers, for whoremongers, for them that defile themselves with mankind, for menstealers, for liars, for perjured persons, and if there be any other thing that is contrary to sound doctrine (1 Tim. 1:9-10).

The law is for such persons. The law was never intended to be something that would help me to live my Christian life. The law is something to show me when I do wrong. A fence along the roadside is a good thing if it is used as a fence, but people do not drive on it. The fence is there to keep travelers from sliding into the ditch. That is the intended purpose of the law. Paul adds that this is "according to the glorious gospel of the blessed

The Purpose of the Gospel

God, which was committed to my trust" (1 Tim. 1:11).

There is something almost magnificent in the way in which Paul makes this statement. He sets forth his affirmation, states the situation as it is, and puts up no argument about himself. He had the authority; he knew in his own heart and mind that he had the truth; so he stated it. It is helpful to notice how Paul bases his interpretation: "according to the glorious gospel of the blessed God, which was committed to my trust." This shows that in interpreting the Bible not every person's idea is valid, but we can be assured the ideas that Paul presented are valid, because he was the authorized spokesman.

Chapter 3

THE LORD'S PART IN SALVATION

Can you understand that to bring a soul to faith in Christ, the Lord Himself must want this and act first?

> And I thank Christ Jesus our Lord, who hath enabled me, for that he counted me faithful, putting me into the ministry; who was before a blasphemer, and a persecutor, and injurious: but I obtained mercy, because I did it ignorantly in unbelief. And the grace of our Lord was exceeding abundant with faith and love which is in Christ Jesus (1 Tim. 1:12-14).

It is the most natural thing for any human being to seek credit for what he has done that is good, and to seek to escape responsibility for what he has done that is bad. Since the blessing of God is good, men naturally want to deserve it, to earn it. It would make them feel so good if they could qualify for the blessing of God. No doubt many turn away from God in despair because they feel they cannot make it. They think there is something to do, and they say to themselves, "I could never be good enough, or I could never do what is good enough." But all this is the result of an error.

The experience of Saul the Pharisee in his conversion serves splendidly as a model for this very truth. Paul could say when he was standing before Agrippa:

> I verily thought with myself, that I ought to do many things contrary to the name of Jesus of Nazareth (Acts 26:9).

Paul, as a young man, was not only without faith in Jesus of Nazareth, but he was willfully opposed to it. He actually thought that he ought to do things contrary to the name of Jesus of Nazareth. Paul's life is an example of the merciful grace of God, who sought Paul when he was opposed to Christ.

The Lord's Part in Salvation

> For ye know the grace of our Lord Jesus Christ, that, though he was rich, yet for your sakes he became poor, that ye through his poverty might be rich (2 Cor. 8:9).

Those are wonderful words, and I would hesitate to add anything to them. But when I quote that passage, I remember I did not ask for that great act of the Lord, nor even look for it.

Paul understood that God planned from eternity for Paul to serve Him.

> But when it pleased God, who separated me from my mother's womb, and called me by his grace, to reveal his Son in me (Gal. 1:15-16).

No doubt Paul had in mind that God was thinking about him before he was born. We can humbly think this is true for each of us. Not only for the great people, not only for the unusual ones, but this is true for everybody. Almighty God had you in mind before you were born, and He had you born exactly where you were. He arranges, in His providence, exactly the circumstances that you are living through. And all the way along God has in mind to lead you to Himself.

The Scriptures show that when God made you, He knew that you should come to Him, and that you should be one of His, in His family. You should be one among the brethren of His Son the Lord Jesus Christ. Now Paul in himself was in darkness, in weakness, in sinfulness as a man, but God had in mind what He could do with Paul. This is what God did: "Who hath enabled me, for that he counted me faithful, putting me into the ministry" (1 Tim. 1:12). God enabled him; Paul knew that he would never, without God's help, have had what it took to be an apostle of the Lord Jesus Christ.

When I hear people talking about Paul, and when I glance into some of the books that are biographies of Paul, I wonder why those authors feel justified in spending all that time pointing out the background of Paul, the training of Paul, and all the things that Paul himself had, as if that was their understanding of why he became the great apostle. Do you realize that Paul never once gave credit to those aspects in accounting for his service as an apostle?

Of course God was involved in where Paul was born and where he was brought up and where he was educated. God was involved in all these things. Paul knew that those various aspects were not the important factors in his life. But Paul said something in Romans 7:18 that clears the air here:

> For I know that in me (that is, in my flesh,) dwelleth no good thing: for to will is present with me; but how to perform that which is good I find not (Rom. 7:18).

If he was to become a believer and an apostle, it was because God enabled him.

No doubt God's enabling is often misunderstood when men become preachers, or persons go as missionaries. We need to remember how Jesus of Nazareth told His apostles:

> Ye have not chosen me, but I have chosen you, and ordained you, that ye should go and bring forth fruit. . . . (John 15:16).

I am satisfied many would say, "Now that would be a good thing for a missionary or preacher to keep in mind." And they would be right. It would be. The fact is, that woman in the house, that mother in the home, did not choose the situation that she is in. She did not choose Almighty God, she did not even choose the Lord Jesus Christ. He chose her and ordained her that she should go and bring forth fruit.

Paul goes on to say about himself: "Who was before a blasphemer." Paul, as Saul the Pharisee, was a sincere person. He could say that he served God from his forefathers with a clear conscience, but he was very wrong. He had all the trouble that a person would have who was intent on going somewhere but was traveling in the wrong direction. I do not need to tell you he would never get there. That was how it was with Paul. Sincerity is not a measure of truth. Obedience is the essence of rightness. It is the person who obeys God who is right.

Paul went on to say, "and a persecutor." In his blindness, in his ignorance, he hurt people while trying to do what he thought was right. He had actually injured other people. He was openly antagonistic to the Gospel. He did great harm. Just as there are people today who are living contrary to the Gospel of Jesus Christ. These really do harm to other people, usually innocent folks, and oftentimes the unlearned.

> . . . but I obtained mercy, because I did it ignorantly in unbelief (1 Tim. 1:13).

God as a gracious, merciful, pitying, compassionate God actually laid hold on Paul. It is true God is gracious, merciful, pitying; and He is compassionate. But we should never forget God is no fool. He knows what He is doing, as He did with Paul.

> And the grace of our Lord was exceeding abundant with faith and love which is in Christ Jesus (1 Tim. 1:14).

Chapter 4

PAUL WAS A PATTERN

Can you understand why it is so important for a person to see in someone else the processes of becoming a believer?

> This is a faithful saying, and worthy of all acceptation, that Christ Jesus came into the world to save sinners; of whom I am chief. Howbeit for this cause I obtained mercy, that in me first Jesus Christ might show forth all longsuffering, for a pattern to them which should hereafter believe on him to life everlasting. Now unto the King eternal, immortal, invisible, the only wise God, be honour and glory for ever and ever. Amen (1 Tim. 1:15-17).

Living as a believer is so very important for both now and forever. It cannot be done by any person in his or her own strength. It is possible by the power of God; but the power of God is effectual only when and where there is faith. Faith is more than just an attitude, or even a willingness or an acceptance. Faith is specifically grasping the promises of God. Therefore faith is basically something which must be learned.

> So then faith cometh by hearing, and hearing by the word of God (Rom. 10:17).

Faith is not only the Word that you hear, but it involves also the meaning and the obeying which comes in responding. But God is invisible, so how can I know Him? How can I see Him to obey Him? What does it mean to obey God? For this I must see manifestations in other believers. A believer can read the Bible with trust and be guided by the Holy Spirit. But how about an unbeliever? How can he ever find out how to become a believer? Paul understood that his own experience was a pattern for others who would come afterwards. He says plainly: "For this cause I obtained mercy." It was definitely in God's plan that Saul the Pharisee should be stopped on the Damascus road, should be convinced and converted by the living Lord Jesus Christ in a moment, and that he should forever after be a faithful servant of the Lord.

Have you ever wondered why you were brought to faith? Why did God give you the capacity to believe in Him? I know He did that for the saving of your soul, but then once done He could have just "swished you away." Why did He leave you here? Paul said, "That in me first Jesus Christ might show forth all longsuffering." To anybody who understood the circumstances, it would be obvious that the way God dealt with Paul showed long-suffering.

Paul was not a perfect man. He had done many things contrary to the name of the Lord Jesus Christ, leaving wrong influences and impressions on other people. The Lord Jesus had suffered in every one of those things. "I am Jesus whom thou persecutest." When Paul was committing the believers to prison, he was injuring the Lord Jesus Christ. No matter how hostile Paul had been, the Lord was meek; and no matter how bitter Paul had been, the Lord was kind and compassionate.

Can we really take these words of Paul's testimony into our hearts? Today there is bitter opposition to the Gospel of the Lord Jesus Christ. Can these opponents, these people who are now so bitter, these people who are now so hostile against Him, can they be saved? You might quickly say, "Yes." But why could you say that? How would you know? Because, you say, the Lord is meek and patient. And that is true. Paul recognized it. The Son of God was always as He is. It was shown in His dealing with Paul.

In telling about the Gospel we often use the testimonies of people who have been far away from God, and then turned around and came to Him. We hear about those who have been addicted to some appetite and have been practically useless as human beings, suddenly being transformed, with their whole hearts and minds being changed. This can happen, and it does happen when people turn to Him.

In the short treatise of the book of Acts, only twenty-eight chapters, and none of them very long, the story of the conversion of the Apostle Paul is repeated three times in detail. I cannot but feel this is the way the Holy Spirit has of emphasizing, "This is what it really means; look at it." For generation after generation people have heard the Gospel and have believed in the Lord Jesus Christ and been saved. What did they believe? They believed that Christ Jesus would receive them. What do you mean by that? The way He received Paul.

> This is a faithful saying, and worthy of all acceptation, that Christ Jesus came into the world to save sinners; of whom I am chief (1 Tim. 1:15).

This is the essence of the Gospel. This is what we preach. Christ Jesus came into the world to seek and to save the lost. Have you ever felt that you were lost? You need not despair. No matter how wicked you have been, no matter how opposed you have been, no matter how negligent you have been, the grace of the Lord Jesus Christ is greater than all your sins. This is the essence of the Gospel message.

When we approach anybody about getting right with God, we start here. We tell him Christ came to save sinners "of whom I am chief." That was Paul's own estimate of himself. By the way, when he calls himself the chief of sinners, the Apostle Paul is not referring to misdeeds on his part. You will remember that he was a man who could say that he had served God, with a clear conscience, from his forefathers, that he "profited in the Jews' religion above many my equals in mine own nation" (Gal. 1:14). Paul had been a moral man. Then why was he the chief of sinners? That is the way he thought about himself; that was his attitude about himself. If you should have the attitude, "There isn't anybody as unworthy as I am," thank the Lord. If you have the feeling, "Sometimes I just wonder if He could even save me," thank the Lord because it shows that you have the right attitude. It is all true just the way you feel and more, but it is also true that He came for you.

Paul ends his personal reference with verse 17. When we read that, let us keep in mind he has been talking about himself. After he has been referring to himself in this way, he writes:

> Now unto the King eternal, immortal, invisible, the only wise God, be honour and glory for ever and ever. Amen (1 Tim. 1:17).

Chapter 5

THE IMPORTANCE OF A GOOD CONSCIENCE

Do you realize that to be blessed of God, a soul must not only believe but also obey?

> This charge I commit unto thee, son Timothy, according to the prophecies which went before on thee, that thou by them mightest war a good warfare; holding faith, and a good conscience; which some having put away concerning faith have made shipwreck: of whom is Hymeneus and Alexander; whom I have delivered unto Satan, that they may learn not to blaspheme (1 Tim. 1:18-20).

Paul was the apostle to the Gentiles, setting forth the Gospel of the grace of God. His teaching is marked by an emphasis upon the freedom that we have from rules and regulations. It is a common thing to say that Paul's Gospel amounted to saying "only believe." He emphasized that Christ Jesus came into the world to save sinners.

It is true that to believe I must admit, but to be complete I must commit. Paul had a clear grasp of this.

> But this I confess unto thee, that after the way which they call heresy, so worship I the God of my fathers, believing all things which are written in the law and in the prophets: and have hope toward God, which they themselves also allow, that there shall be a resurrection of the dead, both of the just and unjust (Acts 24:14-15).

You will notice that he believed, but you will remember he also worshiped God and had hope in the Resurrection. Then he exercised himself to have always a conscience void of offense toward God and toward men. I am not sure that we fully understand what is meant when he wrote to Timothy: "according to the prophecies which went before on thee." It could be that Timothy had been well-spoken of by other people before

Paul asked him to join in his missionary work. Timothy was a true believer. "This charge" refers to what Paul proceeded to outline. Paul gave Timothy advice and admonition to help him do good work in guiding the churches that he had been asked to serve.

"Holding faith, and a good conscience" are two principles that were to be the important emphases in Timothy's ministry. He was to emphasize the importance of faith. This was the most important part of the Gospel message: taking the promises of God as true, as revealed in the Scriptures. When Paul wrote about the faith that saves, and about the faith that the believer is to have, he had in mind the way a believer grasps the promises of God set forth in the Scriptures. He continued, "Which some having put away concerning faith have made shipwreck." Now later he told who these were. They were Hymeneus and Alexander.

It would seem that if a person does not cherish a good conscience, he is liable to suffer shipwreck in exercising his faith. To say "I believe" is good. But then the believer is to live according to that, and he is to act according to faith. In living in faith the believer will be sensitive to the appearance of his actions. He is to conduct himself in a way that is fitting and proper. If a man says he believes in God, he will look to God, he will believe God is almighty, he will believe God is sovereign, he will believe God is before all. Thus in his heart and mind he will honor God. He will reverence God.

The believer will worship God, and this will be seen in his conduct. If he has a good conscience about his faith toward God, he will bow down to God, he will be humble in God's presence. He will walk in the presence of God with fear and trembling. This would show to other people a good conscience.

When a man says that he will do the will of God, he includes being honest and telling the truth. A good conscience would be one that would be void of offense. Apparently faith needs to move within the curb of a good conscience, because when a person says, "I believe," he is not telling how much he knows. He is not saying what he is going to do. He is simply saying from his point of view he believes in God. Then I watch him; and if his conduct is something that fits in with the idea of God, I think he is sincere. But if his conduct is not something

The Importance of a Good Conscience

that fits in with the idea of God, I do not think he is sincere.

I feel Paul meant to say that if a person willfully does wrong, his grasp of Bible truth, that is, his faith, is defective. When a person says he believes the Bible, he means he will obey God. He will be free from what sinful men say to do. He will not pay any attention to what others do. However, if in his conduct he is not carrying out the very simple elements of the law of God: viz., honesty and sincerity, then that person will actually be restating his faith. Somehow or other he will twist his faith in such a way as to allow him to do what he is doing. In this he will be making a mistake. He will come into ruin. "Of whom is Hymeneus and Alexander."

Paul did not hesitate to name the heretics. Commonly speaking and for various reasons we intimate, insinuate, and imply; but we hesitate to say simply, "That man is saying the wrong thing." We are not inclined to do that. Paul did not hesitate to name the heretics, "whom I have delivered unto Satan."

This is another expression of which we are vague in our understanding. This seems to have been taken out of Jewish culture and literature about committing a man, turning him over, to Satan. I think that so far as Paul was concerned, he no longer fellowshiped with Hymeneus and Alexander. He let them go to the devil. That is rather rough, but that is exactly what Paul meant. Paul meant he did not try to protect them nor justify them, "that they may learn not to blaspheme."

Is that what happens when a person lives in sin, but talks the Gospel? Is he actually blaspheming in the sight of God? These are very serious verses. I am drawing attention to them because Paul has written them to Timothy. They should make us conscious of the fact that our daily lives must be consistent with what we believe so that God can bless us.

Chapter 6

PRAYER FOR PUBLIC OFFICIALS

Do you realize the Bible asks every believer to pray for the governor of his state even though that governor may not be a member of any church?

> I exhort therefore, that, first of all, supplications, prayers, intercessions, and giving of thanks, be made for all men; for kings, and for all that are in authority; that we may lead a quiet and peaceable life in all godliness and honesty (1 Tim. 2:1-2).

I sometimes wonder how often those words are ignored. They are so plain. Paul exhorts, which is a little more than just asking. He urges. I do not wonder that people skip this passage. But it is enough to make one stop in his tracks. It seems almost as though Paul knew the present day we are living in.

In the days of Paul there were no kings, nor anyone in authority, who believed in Jesus Christ. Pontius Pilate was not a believer in Jesus Christ. King Agrippa was not a believer in Jesus Christ. Herod was not a believer. And yet Paul says that "supplications, prayers, intercessions, and giving of thanks, be made for all men; for kings." When Paul reminded Timothy that prayer should be made for kings and for all who were in authority, he did not mean for their personal salvation. He was thinking of their official work, their functioning.

You will remember that in Romans 13:1 Paul writes, "For there is no power but of God: the powers that be are ordained of God." The believer where he lives in society, as we are living in this country, has a certain structured government over him. Any state in which we live has a governor, and our country has a president. We are reminded by these words of Paul that God is directly aware of each one of these social situations. One could ask, "If God is involved in all that exists and ordains it, how can

Prayer for Public Officials

there be so much trouble?" God has not promised to make this world a permanent affair. "In the world you shall have tribulation."

Will trouble always bring a man to God? No, not always. Faith is purified by fire. If one has faith, it will be purified by trouble. In this Paul indicates plainly why we should pray:

> I exhort therefore, that, first of all, supplications, prayers, intercessions, and giving of thanks, be made for all men; for kings, and for all that are in authority; that we may lead a quiet and peaceable life in all godliness and honesty (1 Tim. 2:1-2).

This goal may well be new to my own thinking, that this is the whole reason why believers want a good government in the state, and a quiet situation in the country. They want to be able to live a quiet and peaceful life in all godliness and honesty. This purpose may be new to my own thinking, but it is true to the Word of God.

Living a quiet life is apparently not the prerogative of any individual. A person cannot make up his own mind, "I am going to live a quiet life." The neighbors may not let you. That belongs in the providence of God. God can arrange it.

Quiet means no disturbance. If there is to be no disturbance in my community, those disruptive elements must be controlled. Controllers must be persons of authority. They need not be believers, but they must be persons gifted to control. When they perform their task of controlling effectively, God in His providence can affect the conditions of quietness and peace.

In Paul's time there were such persons. You will remember Nicodemus and Cornelius. They were not believers in Christ, yet they conducted themselves with godliness and honesty. Such officials may be doing the will of God even if they are not aware of Him. So we are led to this point, that we pray for all who are in authority for the sake of the common welfare, making supplications by specific requests.

I wonder if you will be prompted to pray for your governor, the mayor of your city, the president of your country? Paul would ask you to do it. You are to pray for those people in authority so that they may control the situation and you will be able to live your life quietly and peaceably in all godliness and honesty. The leader may be acting wrongfully. You and I are to ask God to be gracious to those, even those who ignore Him, that they may be guided better than they know. Now this may well turn out to be short of such persons being saved, even though we would like all men to be saved. As soon as a person is in a public office, you and I should support him so that he may conduct the government to provide quietness and peace. Then we can live with godliness and honesty.

Paul goes on to mention the "giving of thanks." Now you will say, "I just do not see what we can thank God for in connection with this." Well, it might be quite possible that you may not see, and it may be quite possible that I may not see; but let us be humble enough to have in mind that God knows. We are not approving anything, and we are not condemning anybody. We are not passing judgment. We are simply asking that Almighty God would be gracious, and we thank Him for what He has done.

In every situation you should watch, look around you, see where something good has happened, and thank God for it. James says, "Every good gift and every perfect gift is from above, and cometh down from the Father of lights" (James 1:17). I need to get hold of the idea that sometimes things happen that are pretty good, with no credit necessarily to anybody on earth. We can give God the glory that there are such good things happening. We pray to God, and in everything commit ourselves to Him. May the Lord bless our hearts to enable us humbly to be obedient in these matters.

Chapter 7

ONE MEDIATOR

Do you understand what is meant by the saying, "There is one mediator between God and men, the man Christ Jesus"?

> For this is good and acceptable in the sight of God our Saviour; who will have all men to be saved, and to come unto the knowledge of the truth. For there is one God, and one mediator between God and men, the man Christ Jesus; who gave himself a ransom for all, to be testified in due time (1 Tim. 2:3-6).

We ask ourselves, what is it that is good and acceptable in the sight of God our Saviour? Does it not refer to what went before this, namely, "supplications, prayers, intercessions, and giving of thanks, be made for all men"? Is not that good and acceptable in the sight of God? Or does it refer to the second part of that sentence, "that we may lead a quiet and peaceable life in all godliness and honesty"? Would not that be good in the sight of God? It certainly would. What is good and acceptable in the sight of God our Savior is that believing people should pray for those in authority, and that they may lead a quiet and peaceable life in all godliness and honesty.

Let us look at this statement: "Who will have all men to be saved." Does this mean that God will save all men regardless of what they do? Or does this mean that God wants to do this for all men? I have always felt on the basis of this verse that almighty God would have been glad to save anybody and everybody who would come to Him, because He was able to do it. If someone should ask me, "If God wanted to do it, why didn't He just do it?" I would answer, "The fact is God made man in His own image and gave man certain liberty, a certain freedom of choice. While God calls him, promises him, urges him, entices him, and works in every possible way to draw this man to Himself, it would appear that it is the privilege of a human being to make his own choice." Should this then be what God means that He *will* do for all people, regardless, or does it mean that this is what God *wants* to do for all men?

As we continue to look at the question, "If He wants to do it, why doesn't He do it?" let us bring something else to mind. Would you agree that it is God's plan that a man have two eyes? Then what about the man who is blind? Is that God's will for him? You could say it was not His first intention, but you must admit He allowed it to happen. I am inclined to feel that the permissive will of God is one thing, whereas the directive will of God is another. I am inclined to think that God's original plan would have been the normal situation, but He allows and permits things to happen that are contrary to that.

Is it not true that while God may overrule and control, still men make their own choices and choose what they want? When men choose that which is evil, God does not strike them dead on the spot. He works with them, seeking to overcome the evil, but if the thing they chose was evil it will count accordingly. The Scriptures say that every man is going to answer for every deed done in the body. The fact is that for every idle word that he has spoken, man will have to answer to almighty God. Human beings have a certain freedom, and in that freedom they can turn away from God in such a way that they can be lost. There are people who will be lost.

> Enter ye in at the strait gate: for wide is the gate, and broad is the way, that leadeth to destruction, and many there be which go in thereat: because strait is the gate, and narrow is the way, which leadeth unto life, and few there be that find it (Matt. 7:13-14).

That is the way it is revealed in the Bible.

The Scriptures show that God is no respecter of persons. He would have all men to be saved. Because God is no respecter of persons, I should be very careful that I do not play favorites with people. God sees those unbelieving, ungodly neighbors. He sent His Son for them. It may be true they will not accept; it may be true they will stay away; it may be true they will be eternally lost; but we should never forget that so far as God is concerned, He would have all men to be saved.

When you think of the word "save," put the letter "l" in and think of it as the word "salve." This brings in the healing functions. God wants to heal the sores of mankind. He wants to heal the sick. That is what the Lord Jesus did when He was here. Someone may ask: "If almighty God is almighty, why does He allow sickness?" That is something God has not revealed to me. But one thing He did reveal to me: He gave His Son to die for sinners. He, being the gracious God that He is, kind and merciful as He is, can be trusted to overrule and to bring His will to pass for good. When we are thinking in terms of people being brought to God, we should remember ". . . the goodness of God leadeth thee to repentance" (Rom. 2:4). It will be necessary for men to repent, but sinners may be motivated by the kindliness of God, rather than by dire threats of destruction which are certainly sure to come.

There is one Mediator between God and men, the man Christ Jesus. It was in the eternal plan of God that His Son would give Himself to save the creatures of God. Every person living is a creature of God, and God so loved the world that He gave His only begotten Son, that whosoever would believe in Him should not perish but have everlasting life. Now the eternal plan of God from the very first was that His Son would give Himself to save creatures who would put their trust in Him. That eternal plan which was always true became obvious in Jesus of Nazareth.

This passage, therefore, seems to teach very clearly that first a Mediator (a go-between) is needed between man and God. There is a great gulf fixed with man in his sin and God in His holiness. Who is the Mediator? This Mediator is One who understands about men, because He took on a human form Himself; and He understands about God because He is the Son of God. No wonder then that we say only one Mediator is acceptable. The Son of God was in human form, and mediation is on the basis of His shed blood, His death. The perfect example of a perfect life would not have been enough to save my soul. I was doomed to die and someone needed to take my place and needed to die in my place. I read in the Bible this wonderful news, "Who gave himself a ransom for all." We like to remember that, because of what He did, the call is open, "Whosoever will may come."

Chapter 8

PAUL'S BASIC EMPHASIS

Do you ever get the idea that only good people and important people should pray?

> Whereunto I am ordained a preacher, and an apostle, (I speak the truth in Christ, and lie not;) a teacher of the Gentiles in faith and verity. I will therefore that men pray every where, lifting up holy hands, without wrath and doubting (1 Tim. 2:7-8).

These marvelous words indicate the understanding and the purpose of the Apostle Paul. When he says "whereunto" he refers back to what he has been talking about in verses 3, 4, and 5. He says unto this testimony he was ordained a preacher. He was set aside for this purpose and assigned to do this thing.

In parentheses we read, "I speak the truth in Christ, and lie not," meaning, "I am giving it to you honestly and openly and plainly." The Apostle Paul did not feel that he would appear conceited when he said that he was a preacher and an apostle. He knew he had a terrific responsibility, but he understood his call to this end. He had just stated that the purpose of God was to have all men be saved and come to the knowledge of truth. In this context Paul had been ordained a preacher and an apostle. Paul understood his call was toward achieving this goal.

The word "ordained" means "prepared for," or "set aside unto." It was as though almighty God had taken this man Saul the Pharisee and said about him: "Give him to me, I want to use him. I have a job for him." Paul was ordained, set aside, prepared for this particular thing, that he was to preach and teach the Gospel of the Lord Jesus Christ.

A preacher states the promise of God and urges people to believe it. A preacher does more than tell. This is where you can feel the difference between preaching and teaching. A teacher need not be limited to telling; but when we speak about teaching, we are thinking primarily about informing, telling. When we speak about preaching, we are referring to an activity in which a person is primarily urging, pushing, trying to get his message over, exhorting. When we speak about an "apostle" we mean someone who is authorized to define the message. Paul can say what the Gospel really means, and Paul's words are authentic.

Paul goes on to say, "I speak the truth in Christ, and lie not." Here again Paul reiterates his claim to honesty, which is an important trait in any witness to the Lord Jesus Christ. Above everything else a witness should be honest. I am using the word "witness" in the broadest sense, but this would be especially true of a preacher.

Someone might ask: "What might he lie about? What would there be to lie about?" Some things he could not lie about. He could not lie about the presence of Jesus of Nazareth here on earth. Everybody knew about that. He could not lie about the works of Jesus of Nazareth, healing of the sick, opening the eyes of the blind, making the lame walk, and even raising Lazarus from the dead. That was known to hundreds and hundreds of people. There was no chance of lying about that. He could not lie about the death of the Lord Jesus Christ. A whole multitude saw Jesus die. He could not lie about the burial of the Lord Jesus Christ, because people saw Jesus put in the grave, the stone rolled in place and sealed, and the soldiers put in front. No, He was really dead. Then what could Paul lie about?

The truth in Christ is more than the bare historic facts. For example, Christ was the Son of God. That fact was not something visible, but this is one thing Paul would say. Paul told the truth when he said that Christ died for our sins. But that would not appear visibly on the cross. Those thieves who died on either side did not die for our sins. There was no physical way in which you could see that. But the Apostle Paul said it, and preached it, and told the world that when Christ Jesus died on Calvary's cross He carried our sins away. Paul preached that Christ rose from the dead. There were many people who saw that (at one time as many as five hundred brethren), there were numbers of persons from time to time in the forty days after His resurrection who saw Him; but the great multitude of the population did not see Him. However, Paul went from place to place alleging and affirming that Jesus of Nazareth had been raised from the dead. About this Paul could say "I did not lie. I told the truth." Christ's death was seen, that He died on Calvary. Everybody could see that. The fact that He rose from the dead was hard to believe. I know the grave was empty and the testimony was there, but people can doubt when they do not want to believe. That was the case even with Paul's testimony.

Then Paul would tell people that Jesus of Nazareth was seen after He was raised from the dead. He was alive, and He ascended into heaven in full view of dozens of people. More than a hundred people saw Him go into the heavens right there in front of their eyes. This is what Paul said, but people would doubt him. Now Paul said, "I am telling you the truth." That Christ is now in the presence of God interceding for us, you could never see. There was no way of establishing that fact, but Paul declared it.

He also declared that Jesus of Nazareth, being raised from the dead and being glorified in the presence of God, sent forth His Holy Spirit into the believer at the time of Pentecost. No one ever saw the Spirit and no one has seen Him move, but Paul said that the Holy Spirit would be in the believers. God sent the Spirit forth into their hearts to live in them.

Paul did not hesitate to say over and over again that this same Jesus would so return in like manner as they had seen Him go, and that He will take believers to Himself. This is the truth in Christ that Paul was preaching.

He was a teacher of the Gentiles. I told you that a preacher is one who urges, but a teacher is one who explains. Paul explained things. A preacher presents the authorized message, an apostle defines the authentic message, and a teacher explains the message.

Primarily the meaning of the word "Gentile" is one who is not a Jew. What does that mean? In Paul's day a Gentile would be a person who had no acquaintance with the Scriptures, and no acquaintance with the sacraments. Gentiles were people who simply did not know what the Bible taught; and who did not know the ways in which the people of God worshiped Him. To Gentiles the whole truth needed to be explained. When Paul was teaching in faith, what was he doing? He was teaching them what to believe, what to expect. The word "verity" means the actual truth: what will happen and what God will do.

"I will therefore that men pray every where" (1 Tim. 2:8). Not as a class, men as over against women; but as human beings, men, women, and children having communion with God in prayer. Offering praise, giving thanks, making petitions everywhere, any place, any time, "lifting up holy hands, without wrath and doubting." This is the conduct that the Apostle Paul felt was desirable. He urged Timothy to have this in mind because of the truth that the Apostle Paul preached. He wanted human beings everywhere to turn to God, to draw nigh unto Him, and to lift up holy hands without wrath and doubting, praying to God.

Chapter 9

PROPER DRESS FOR A WOMAN

Can you understand why it matters how a woman dresses?

> In like manner also, that women adorn themselves in modest apparel, with shamefacedness and sobriety; not with braided hair, or gold, or pearls, or costly array; but (which becometh women professing godliness) with good works (1 Tim. 2:9-10).

These were the words of the Apostle Paul, an older preacher as he wrote to Timothy, a younger preacher who was to have the responsibility of leading a congregation of believers. Paul knew that Timothy would be called upon to define for his people the things that are proper and the things that are improper, the things that are wise and the things that are unwise. By writing, "In like manner also," Paul referred to what he had written before. In that previous verse were recorded the remarkable words of Paul, "I will therefore that men pray every where, lifting up holy hands, without wrath and doubting." Now Paul went right on, "In like manner also," implying that what he was going to write to the women was similar in significance to what he had written to the men. In each case he was guiding believers into such conduct as would be appropriate, proper, helpful in their witnessing for the Lord.

It is a common practice to imply that Paul was a "woman-hater." Such an idea comes from the critic's own mind. If anybody offers guidance to someone in the way of saying, "Do it like this, and do not do it like that," it is not meant to imply that the people who are being instructed are inferior. Not at all. We could miss the blessing of what Paul is saying if we feel he thinks certain persons are inferior.

By way of showing that Paul is not alone in what he has to say, let me call your attention to what Peter has written. He has just spoken about wives and then says:

> Whose adorning let it not be that outward adorning of plaiting the hair, and of wearing of gold, or of putting on of apparel; but let it be the hidden man of the heart, in that which is not corruptible, even the ornament of a meek and quiet spirit, which is in the sight of God of great price. For after this manner in the old time the holy women also, who trusted in God, adorned themselves, being in subjection unto their own husbands (1 Peter 3:3-5).

Peter based his remarks on the testimony and the practices of godly women in the history of God's people.

When we are thinking about this and about the Gospel being addressed to women, it would be well for us to recognize there is a natural difference in human beings. There is a natural difference between men and women, and that difference is recognized in Scripture. Do you realize that men and women have different outlooks, and young people are still different? Let me put it to you this way. I would say that men are interested in performance. A man feels good when he is doing something, and he feels better if he is doing it well. He is probably never so pleased or satisfied as when he is telling a woman about what he has done, because this really makes him feel good. Women are interested in their appearance, and may I say to you that this is normal. The woman's attitude can be expressed in the question, "How do I look?" I am sure in my own mind that if you find a woman who is not interested in that, she is sick. Such an interest in a woman is normal. Young people are interested in what folks think of them, far more than how they do or what they look like. Their big question even among themselves is, "How do I rate? What do others think of me?" The Scriptures are suited to each class. They tell a man what to do, the woman how to look, and the young person how to really amount to something. The Bible does not deny human differences, nor does the Bible condemn these differences. Actually the Bible leads us to fulfill each of these outlooks as a normal, natural, wholesome, healthy expectation for each one in such a way as to honor God. To summarize, I can say quickly men are to pray, women are to be modest, and young people are to be ambitious to be well-pleasing to God.

In like manner also Paul goes on to say in effect that a

woman's modest humility is to match a man's piety. God sees them both. "That women adorn themselves" to be seen? I say, of course. Their conduct sets the stage. The way in which they act can actually point to the presence of God. At a time of social confusion, such as occurs for instance in a time of war, the fashions of women's dress are extreme. Go back in history, and if you have lived long enough to live through several wars, you may know this from your own observation.

Now notice "that women shall adorn themselves in modest apparel." By the way, the Bible outlines no definite style of clothing. It is the way the clothes are worn that matters. The Bible talks about the way you conduct yourself. "With shamefacedness and sobriety" is a direct reference to the frame of mind, not to how much cloth, where it is applied, or where it is put on the body. It means being conscious of one's responsibility to look proper, and with a keen sense of anything that would make one ashamed. "Not with braided hair, or gold, or pearls, or costly array"; these things are not necessarily evil per se. It is only when confidence is put in them as a basis for acceptance before God and man, that they are to be counted as being evil or misleading. I know there are people who on the basis of this Bible passage will not wear any jewelry. I would like to ask them very gently, do they wear expensive clothes? Will they do such a thing as buy costly dresses on occasion? Would they wear an expensive suit? You know there are times and occasions when that is proper. Is it evil? No. It is only evil when those things are done as if you were to offer yourself for acceptance. It is when confidence is put in these things that they are in themselves misleading.

"But with good works," as we read in Peter, so Paul says the same thing. Women are to cover themselves with good works, which becometh women who profess godliness. In the next study we will note more about Paul's dealing with the role of women. In this Scripture we are interested in the dress. It matters how a woman appears to other people, because she is also visible to God. Any person conscious of the presence of God and acting accordingly will dress properly.

Chapter 10

THE STATUS OF WOMAN

Do you ever get the impression that the Bible teaches that woman was created to live on a lower status than man?

> Let the woman learn in silence with all subjection. But I suffer not a woman to teach, nor to usurp authority over the man, but to be in silence. For Adam was first formed, then Eve. And Adam was not deceived, but the woman being deceived was in the transgression. Notwithstanding she shall be saved in childbearing, if they continue in faith and charity and holiness with sobriety (1 Tim. 2:11-15).

Do the Scriptures really teach that woman belongs at a lower level than man? While we are thinking about that, we should note several general observations. In the world, women are commonly abused. I do not think anybody will question that statement. In one culture after another woman evidently is given a lesser place.

About the turn of the century there developed what we call the "romantic" view of woman in which woman was idealized. She was considered a superior person. Comparing a man with a woman always meant that the man came off worse in the comparison. This romantic view of woman, which is in literature and which is set out in philosophy, was not popular with the people by and large. Over the world as a whole it was not practical, and it is not true, actually. In contemporary culture, right now, there is a strong feministic tone, which seems far different from the Bible. The "woman's lib" movement moves on another basis altogether.

To hold that the Bible belittles woman is an error. It is simply not true. As a matter of history where the Gospel has gone, woman has been liberated. It is true that woman has been pushed down in many ways, and has suffered many times because of an inferior social status, but it should not be true where the Gospel is known.

What does Paul actually teach? Is he consistent in what he has to say? He uses the expression "neither male nor female: for ye are all one in Christ Jesus" (Gal. 3:28). Paul would feel so far as the individual soul is concerned that the acceptability before God does not depend upon whether that soul is a man or a woman. So in this passage in 1 Timothy, it looks as though woman is given an inferior place, but this is more apparent than real.

No doubt Paul would say that a woman should accommodate herself in a subordinate role where men and women are working together, but the Son of God does that, too. He accommodates Himself to a subordinate role. Paul wrote the simple statement, "For the husband is the head of the wife" (Eph. 5:23). This is an arrangement which makes the marriage relationship possible and helps it to work out in a peaceful way. It is obviously operative in the domestic living of married people, and that is the only place where it would be meaningful. This statement that the husband is head of the wife would have no bearing on an unmarried woman, and would have no bearing on an unmarried man. Paul does admonish believing women to dress like women and to act like women; but he also admonishes men to dress and act like men.

Now there seems no doubt that in the society of Corinth, woman's role in pagan religion was largely associated with evil. It had a bad odor so far as the public was concerned. Paul refers to such people doing things that were not worthy to be mentioned, and he avoided talking about them in detail. I shall do likewise but we will keep in mind it was really true. This was very much like his advice about dress when he advised how a woman should dress. He described and discussed how a woman in Corinth should dress, but then he ended by saying ". . . we have no such custom, neither the churches of God" (1 Cor. 11:16). By this he was saying that he was not going to insist upon this. I would like to do the same and say we are not going to imply that it has got to be this way. I am just giving you my opinion of the way in which it would work out well.

But when we look more specifically at what Paul wrote, for instance, "Let the woman learn in silence with all subjection"

The Status of Woman

(1 Tim. 2:11), we should remember that he probably meant no arguments in public, no open disputing or abuse in public. Paul thought that would not look good. He had the same feeling about saying it would not look good as he would have said if someone were to appear in public indecently clothed. So far as Paul is concerned, I am quite sure it would not be news to him that a baby is born without clothes, but there is something about the way in which responsible persons conduct themselves. The man who is properly clothed is honoring those around him. The woman who is decently clothed is respecting the people with her; and she would be respecting the very presence of God. Paul would feel that this practice of listening and seeking to understand without argument, would be as proper in its way as being properly dressed would be in its way.

Paul goes on to write,

> But I suffer not a woman to teach, nor to usurp authority over the man, but to be in silence (1 Tim. 2:12).

Here again he may well be thinking about a mixed audience, a situation in which Bible truth is being presented and possibly discussed. Paul would favor that the women should not take any open part in this discussion to the point where they would be differing with men, and would actually be pointing out things contrary to men. Paul would feel that would not have a good flavor. When Paul says for example, "I suffer not a woman to teach," that would be in public. Sometimes the local culture, people in the community, will allow a woman the liberty and freedom to discuss things with a man; but in some places she would not be given this opportunity. Paul teaches that a believer ought to be sensitive to what people in the community approve.

We have women Sunday school teachers, and sometimes these women Sunday school teachers teach in mixed classes. There is nothing objectionable about that, and there is no reason to raise any question about it. We have women missionaries. Paul would say as long as no one asks any questions, believers can go right ahead with what they are doing. Those who do not wish to elect women to public office have strong grounds for thinking it is unwise for women to dispute over spiritual things in public.

> For Adam was first formed, then Eve. And Adam was not deceived, but the woman being deceived was in the transgression (1 Tim. 2:13-14).

This seems to reveal, in comparing men and women, that a certain spiritual instability exists in woman. I am not going to argue the point. I just have a feeling deep down in my heart that there are spiritually minded women who would say, "Amen." That is exactly what they would understand. This puts the responsibility on the man, and that is where it belongs.

> Notwithstanding she shall be saved in childbearing, if they continue in faith and charity and holiness with sobriety (1 Tim. 2:15).

I do not think this means she will be saved by childbearing, but that in childbearing she will have sorrow and grief and she can have the help of God during that time when she is in close fellowship with God. Paul is assuring any woman that she can be delivered from sin by her faith in God, if she continues in faith and charity and holiness with sobriety. This can be expected when she is responsible in public attitudes and public contacts.

Chapter 11

THE PATTERN OF A GOOD ELDER

Can you understand why an elder should be especially careful to be godly in his public conduct?

> This is a true saying, If a man desire the office of a bishop, he desireth a good work. A bishop then must be blameless, the husband of one wife, vigilant, sober, of good behaviour, given to hospitality, apt to teach; not given to wine, no striker, not greedy of filthy lucre; but patient, not a brawler, not covetous (1 Tim. 3:1-3).

The Bible reveals that it is the plan of God that in every group of believers some should be responsible leaders. Among the believers, some are going to be leaders of others. Not all believers are at the same stage of understanding or of dedication. They do not have the same age so far as their life is concerned. Not all believers are at the same stage of understanding, dedication, or of ability.

Believers should grow in grace and in understanding, just as they should grow in obedience. Some people have not grown much, but it is God's plan that they should grow. In all growing they would be responding to the revelation of God's will. What we see in word and in deed in other believers who know and who obey, should lead us in our knowledge and in our obedience. Such leaders in the Bible are called apostles, bishops, and deacons.

"Bishop" in the Greek language is a word that implies an "overseer." It designates someone who has responsibility over, who takes the oversight of people. Actually it is the same word that is used for "shepherd." The shepherd is the person who has oversight of the flock. Some individual believers are given the grace to exercise this function for other believers, to keep them in mind, to oversee their activities, and to give them advice and guide them as they go along in what they are doing.

"A bishop then must be blameless." I know that in some churches the word "bishop" refers to a person of a certain ecclesiastical rank; but the word "bishop" when used in the New Testament did not mean rank, because the church was not organized in that fashion at that time. Since then it has been organized, and we have certain officers defined with certain names. Some communions today have officers that are called bishops. Some of us do not have such officers. So far as my own communion is concerned, the church to which I belong, we speak of "elders." What does Paul describe? How does he picture the character of a bishop or an elder, a leader? He says very simply and plainly a bishop must be blameless. This does not mean that the elder must be sinless; this does not mean he must never have done anything wrong. But I am quite sure that it does mean that he should not allow any aspect of his behavior to be blameable.

The elder certainly would not have any unconfessed sin. His conduct must be such that he is willing to repent of the sin and to make the wrong right. His attitude must be such that no blame is attached to him. The elder must be blameless in his conduct.

"The husband of one wife" would mean at least that he should have one wife at a time. For instance, in this connection the question could be asked: could an unmarried man be an elder? Suppose a man had never married, could he be an elder? I think so, because Paul spoke of himself as being someone who was not leading a wife (1 Cor. 9:5). I appreciate the fact that some folk think that Paul was probably married, that he was either a widower or his wife was not traveling with him, but no one can prove any one of those things about Paul. It is quite obvious that when Paul was writing to the Corinthians he left the impression that he was living alone, he was living a single life at that time. Could an unmarried man be an elder? Yes, I think so. Could a remarried man, a widower, be an elder? Because he had one wife and she died, then he had another wife, is that man then disqualified because he had two wives in the course of his lifetime? Of course not.

The meaning does not seem so clear when we ask: could a

divorced man be an elder? I think that where this is concerned, it would imply again that the man is to have a relationship that has integrity in it, with one woman. Could a divorced man be an elder? Certainly there are such men like that. Some denominations will not allow it, but some do. Could a remarried divorced man be an elder? Any man who has once been divorced might very well question whether or not he should be an elder, whether he should accept the office. Also if a man has been remarried, he could begin to think about this passage. I have known cases of men who were remarried and divorced men who were good elders so far as could be seen from their testimony.

Now let us ask another question, could a woman be an elder? Certainly a woman could not be the husband of one wife, so could she be an elder? There are people who think so, as you know, and in recent years a good many different churches have begun to ordain women as elders. Then what would this mean? Apparently the norm was that of a man serving in this capacity, but I am not sure that the Bible would rule out the other. In any case I think the emphasis is on the idea of family integrity. This I believe in a general way should cover the case.

"Vigilant" means watchful, careful, alert to danger. A man who gets to be an elder should not be foolish. "Sober" means grave, serious-minded, not frivolous, taking a sober view of things. "Of good behavior" is as it sounds. The life style of the elder in the community should be good. He should have a good reputation. When you say "good" you might keep in mind we mean good for something. When a man is of good behavior, it is not just negatively that nothing is wrong, but positively something is actually right. He does the right thing. The community is better off having him than it would be without him.

"Given to hospitality" means ready to entertain strangers. "Apt to teach" is disposed to try and help other people understand. "Not given to wine, no striker" means he is not violent, he does not shake his fists to enforce his argument. "Not greedy of filthy lucre" lays emphasis upon that adjective "filthy." I believe this means the elder should not be greedy for money that is gotten in ways that are wrong, not greedy for gain that is to be made by sharp dealing. An elder is not that kind of man. "But patient" is persistent, consistent, steadfast in his attitude.

"Not a brawler" means that he is not given to contentious conflict, and "not covetous" means "not money-mad."

When you check this description we have just discussed, much of it was negative; but it was negative in the way you make a sketch by drawing on a sheet of paper. The outline of the picture indicates that inside is the likeness of what I am pointing out. What Paul has written about the requirements of a bishop is a picture, a portrait, of a humble, obedient, godly man.

Chapter 12

THE IMPORTANCE OF A GOOD REPUTATION

Does it make a difference when the officers in a congregation are above reproach in their public conduct?

> One that ruleth well his own house, having his children in subjection with all gravity; (for if a man know not how to rule his own house, how shall he take care of the church of God?) Not a novice, lest being lifted up with pride he fall into the condemnation of the devil. Moreover he must have a good report of them which are without; lest he fall into reproach and the snare of the devil (1 Tim. 3:4-7).

These are the words with which the Apostle Paul continues to describe the qualifications of a bishop or an elder. The Bible reveals that God plans for His people to live in companies, in groups. There is no plan in Scripture for any individual to live alone. It is not good for man to be alone. God has set His people in families and in groups. Individuals in a group are not always of the same age, and they are not always of the same capacity. Not everybody in the church is alike. Among the believers a mutual regard should prevail. They were given the new commandment that they should love one another, and for all practical purposes God has given gifts to the congregation in the way of certain specialties. He gave some to be apostles, and some to be prophets, some to be evangelists, some to be pastors and teachers. These people were to promote spiritual growth and life among all believers.

In addition to the spiritual needs of the congregation, there would be practical needs. When a group of people is together, living together and working together, there must be some order in the situation. For this there must be some leadership. We remember the word that says, "How can two walk together except they be agreed?" Certainly if there is difficulty in getting two walking together, there will be more difficulty when ten are walking together, or twenty, or fifty, or even more. It becomes obvious that believers will need leadership.

The Scripture tells us that God gave gifts of healing, of helps, of government. Now helps and governments are functions in the matter of the activities and of the performances of the people. The early church had the apostles. When confusion arose in the church because of unevenness in the distribution of charity, Peter, speaking for the apostles, directed the congregation to select men with certain qualifications who would be appointed to supervise the distribution. These were afterwards called "deacons."

The general word that we translate as "elder" is sometimes translated "bishop," which means "overseer." The Greek word for "deacon" implies "a servant or minister" from which we get "diaconate." The Bible speaks in a general way of the elders as undershepherds, and speaks of the deacons as ministers, servants. It is customary in the organization of believers even to this day that we have bishops, we have elders, we have deacons, etc., various titles being given to certain persons. These are the leaders in the flock. Each denomination has its own procedure for selecting its leaders. Apparently the selection of such leaders, to be recognized by the group, was to be supervised by the apostle as we have it recorded in the sixth chapter of the Book of Acts.

Now we are going to consider Paul's guidance for Timothy in the selection of the leaders, especially the bishops.

> One that ruleth well his own house, having his children in subjection with all gravity (1 Tim. 3:4).

This does not mean so much that he acts as a boss, rather it is a matter that he is doing it well. "Having his children in subjection with all gravity" does not mean that his children are frightened of him, or that he rules them with a hand of terror, but that he is in control. The apostle goes on to say,

> For if a man know not how to rule his own house, how shall he take care of the church of God? (1 Tim. 3:5).

This means to say that there is something constant about leadership. This shows up in experience, in most cases.

In verse 6, "Not a novice" means that no one should be

placed in a responsible position who has not had some experience in the group. "Lest being lifted up with pride," means that a person can become proud because he knows that it is an important thing to be chosen to lead. A person does have a feeling of some importance in being selected, and that is a temptation to pride. Paul comments that when a person is lifted up in pride he could fall into condemnation of the devil. We can always remember that pride goes before a spiritual fall. By becoming proud, one actually leaves himself open to the enemy's way of doing things, and thus he would fall into the condemnation of the devil.

The next verse has something else to say: "Moreover he must have a good report of them which are without." The elder is to be a person with a good reputation. He is to be well-spoken of in the community. He must have a good report from those who are outside the church, "lest he fall into reproach and the snare of the devil." There is far more to a good reputation than just a certificate of his own piety. A good reputation says about a man that people can trust him. If a man does not have a good reputation in a place of leadership he can fall into reproach and the snare of the devil.

Chapter 13

REQUIREMENTS FOR A DEACON

Should there be any difference in the style of living between a deacon and an elder?

> Likewise must the deacons be grave, not doubletongued, not given to much wine, not greedy of filthy lucre; holding the mystery of the faith in a pure conscience. And let these also first be proved; then let them use the office of a deacon, being found blameless (1 Tim. 3:8-10).

As you read the opening part of this third chapter, everything said about a bishop is to apply to a deacon. This brings to mind an interesting fact that, although the deacon has a lesser position as far as status is concerned, he has the same kind of responsibility as far as witnessing is concerned. He is a representative of the Gospel.

Everything that was said about a bishop ought to apply to a deacon. For instance we read, "not given to much wine"; that means not addicted to the use of alcoholic liquors. A deacon might drink some, but not be given to it; he should not be addicted to it. He is no striker, not a violent person, not a person who immediately wants to settle any argument with his fists. He is not greedy for filthy lucre: not a person who is anxious to make money by any means, fair or foul. He is patient: the kind of person who would be faithful through to the end. He is not a brawler, not contentious, not quarrelsome; and not covetous, which means to say not grabby; not a person who is out to get everything he can. Paul said to Timothy, "Likewise must the deacons be grave." When the word "grave" is used, the idea is brought out that he is to be serious-minded, not shifty, but reliable, responsible, good. "Not doubletongued" refers to persons who say one thing one time

Requirements for a Deacon

and another thing another time. They talk one way to one group of people and another way to another group of people. No, the deacons are to be men who are steady, reliable persons who can be trusted anywhere.

It is interesting to note that where the elder was spoken of, Paul said, "not given to wine," but here with the deacon he said, "not given to much wine." This is to say it is quite possible that the deacon might drink some occasionally, but he would not be a heavy drinker. "Not greedy of filthy lucre" implies that this is more than just a person not interested in money; this is a person who is above wanting to make money under any circumstances, fair or foul. A characteristic of this person is that he is careful about his business affairs.

"Holding the mystery of the faith in a pure conscience" brings to mind an emphasis upon inner convictions, upon how a person would feel in his heart. Are you clear in your mind what the mystery of the faith is? The word "mystery" means the hidden truth. What is the hidden truth in the Gospel? If a person is a believer, what is the "mystery of faith" in that man? The Christian truth that is in the heart of the believer is hidden from ungodly men. Having this truth, "Christ in you the hope of glory," the person who is aware of the indwelling Lord Jesus Christ, has found Who is the hidden source of his faith.

When you come in contact with an officer of the church you have a right to expect that there will be something about him that does not appear on the surface. He will be guided by a light which will shine from within him, that nobody else sees. He does not put on any act; he is genuinely what he claims to be. The deacon's life is to be featured by a hidden, unseen, but real relationship with Christ. I hope that in your own fellowship you know men and women who, as you get to know them, and see them, and hear them, and watch them, show that they are inwardly guided to do the right thing, the good thing. They are inwardly helped to be faithful and steadfast and strong and upright at all times, with no deceit. Oh, they may not be perfect. They may make mistakes, but there need be no question about their sincerity nor genuineness.

"And let these also first be proved." This word "proved" means tested, examined. They are to be tried, investigated, and proved before they are asked to be deacons. They should be given other jobs in the church as a test of their character and their ability. A church should be careful not to put into a place of responsibility somebody who has had no experience. Just because a man means well, and just because he is genuine and sincere is not quite enough. Has he had any experience, and how would he get this experience? Give him other jobs to do; give him small jobs to do. If he shows himself to be a faithful man, he is qualifying. If it turns out in the testing, examining, investigating, and looking over his past record, he is found to be above reproach, then let him serve as an officer of the church. Someone may say, "That is mighty strict; that is mighty tight." Yes, but this is a strict business, this is a tight business. We are interested in the saving of souls. We want to bring men to God.

Paul is emphasizing the great care that is proper to make sure that the image of a witness, the person who is standing up for the Gospel, should be kept true. It does make a difference what people say about the leader in the congregation. It is extremely important that the officer of the church, whether he is a deacon or an elder or a minister, should stand up straight, be reliable and sincere, so that he can be counted as being faithful and true. This is very, very important for the sake of the Gospel of the Lord Jesus Christ.

Chapter 14

MORE ABOUT DEACONS

Can you understand why the reputation of a prospective officer in the congregation would be a valid basis upon which to judge his fitness for that office?

The word "deacon" means "minister." It is a word that refers to being like a servant. The deacon is seen in public as an example. People see him as a walking illustration of the Gospel of Jesus Christ. The people in the world have a right to expect that. He claims to belong to those who believe in the living Lord, and so in his life there should be such evidence as would encourage people to believe that he is genuinely sincere about what he has to say.

In addition to the full schedule of requirements that have been set out for elders and for deacons, as well as certain inner qualities that a person must have and certain outward traits or characteristics that he must show, there are some further items to be noticed.

> Even so must their wives be grave, not slanderers, sober, faithful in all things, let the deacons be the husbands of one wife, ruling their children and their own houses well. For they that have used the office of a deacon well purchase to themselves a good degree, and great boldness in the faith which is in Christ Jesus (1 Tim. 3:11-13).

Someone may say, "You mean to tell me that it matters about the wife of a deacon?" Yes, it does. "The wife of an elder?" Yes. "The wife of a minister, of a preacher?" Yes, it matters about her. Someone may say, "We called the preacher. We did not call his wife." But when you called the preacher, his wife was there. That preacher and his wife are one, and when you went to call the preacher you should have had a good look at his wife. It does make a difference.

When you are electing a man to be an elder it makes a difference about his wife, and the apostle Paul indicates here:

> Even so must their wives be grave, not slanderers, sober, faithful in all things (1 Tim. 3:11).

Now what do these words mean? The women likewise must be worthy of respect, not gossipers. Gossip hurts so many churches and so many people. Persons who are in places of responsibility are trusted. Others trust them, and when those you trust talk about you, that is distressing. Consider the average church member. If he ever finds out that the wife of the deacon, elder, or preacher repeated anything to that member's disadvantage, it cuts him to the heart. I can appreciate just now someone may say, "But suppose she is telling the truth?" There is more to it than just telling the truth. Sometimes the truth is such that you should not mention it. You remember the story of Ham, Noah's son, who found his father lying naked in the tent? Noah was lying naked, that was true; and all Ham did was go out and tell the truth. But in this Ham put himself down forever. Ham lost out, his children lost out, his grandchildren lost out, because of his lack of respect and his lack of charity. There is truth about which you should be quiet. You are not God. If you want to pray about persons who have done wrong, go ahead and do that. You can open your heart and open your mouth talking to God. But when it comes to talking to people, it is a matter to be noticed here that the wife of a deacon is not to be a gossiper, nor a slanderer. "Faithful in all things" means full of faith, not just steady but continuing to do what she is supposed to be doing, and believing in God in all things.

"Let the deacons be the husbands of one wife" (1 Tim. 3:12). Again let me suggest humbly, one wife at a time. In other words, the domestic life should stand up under examination, and it should present a clear testimony. "Ruling their children and their own houses well" means "ruling" in the sense of managing. Managing well is possible when the families are happy and obedient. When the general control of the family life is intelligent, and persistent in pointing toward every good thing, and consistent day in and day out, it does not mean the children will never do wrong, and that there will never be any tension or contention in that home. It does mean that the management will be handled well so that the family will be inclined to live together in happy, obedient fashion.

> For they that have used the office of a deacon well purchase to themselves a good degree, and great boldness in the faith which is in Christ Jesus (1 Tim. 3:13).

What is the meaning of such "purchase"? Those who perform well as deacons acquire a good standing for themselves, gain much confidence personally, and much freedom and boldness in the faith which is to be found in Christ. "Purchase" means that they secure, but not with money. Simon the sorcerer in Samaria offered money for blessing, and you will remember Peter told him that he was not right in the sight of God for trying to buy it. Those who do well as deacons will be rewarded by the respect that other people give them, and also by the development of confidence in their own boldness in trusting the Lord. Those who serve well as deacons gain a good standing for themselves among the people, and they develop a great confidence in the faith which is in Christ Jesus.

To be sure, being a deacon is a lesser position. It is not as prominent as being an elder or a minister, but it promises much. It could be said to anybody at a point like this, "Thou hast been faithful in little, I will make thee ruler of much." So we see that so far as the deacon is concerned, in serving and in ministering, his faithfulness will lead him through experiences in praying and in yielding, where he will grow in grace and in knowledge and become strong in the Lord. I could in my own heart and mind pray for every person who holds any office at all in any church. Let us be faithful to any trust that is given to us, and walk humbly and softly before God that we may be blessed.

Chapter 15

THE MYSTERY OF GODLINESS

Do you understand why a believer lives a godly life?

All our interest in the Gospel draws our attention to personal conduct. "How does he do? How consistent is he? How long will he keep it up?" These are the questions we ask when we hear that a person has accepted Christ, and the world would call him a Christian. How would people know? Why would they say it? Because he acts like a Christian. This leads people to conclude he is a Christian. It makes a difference how I do and what I do and the way I do it. But when a person is living in faith, he will often not be conscious of anything special about his conduct.

> These things write I unto thee, hoping to come unto thee shortly: but if I tarry long, that thou mayest know how thou oughtest to behave thyself in the house of God, which is the church of the living God, the pillar and ground of the truth. And without controversy great is the mystery of godliness: God was manifest in the flesh, justified in the Spirit, seen of angels, preached unto the Gentiles, believed on in the world, received up into glory (1 Tim. 3:14-16).

The epistle of Paul to Timothy is packed with sound advice for daily conduct. "These things write I unto thee, hoping to come unto thee shortly." Letter writing is not the best means of communication. Face to face is much better, but I can tell you right now when you cannot be face to face, letters help. This letter will help us to understand the function of the Bible.

One could say that the Bible is God's letter to man. Reading the letter is good, but face to face communion is better. Because of the function of the Holy Spirit, believers do not have to wait until they die and their bodies are laid to rest in a cemetery to see Him face to face. By faith we can walk in His presence daily. But letters are important, and just so, Bible reading is important. The Bible was written for us to lead us into His presence.

> But if I tarry long, that thou mayest know how thou oughtest to behave thyself in the house of God (1 Tim. 3:15).

Paul wanted Timothy to have guidance in practical matters. But did not Timothy have the Holy Spirit? Yes. Would not the Holy Spirit guide? Yes. Well, if he had the Holy Spirit guiding him, would he need any help? In his understanding of God, Timothy would not need any help. "You need no man to teach you." However, with reference to daily conduct, what he should do in his city, what he should do in his family, in his neighborhood, in all such practical affairs, yes, he could use help. Even if a person is spiritual he can always profit by advice from people who know, who have been over the road.

Do you realize what you need in order to benefit by other people's advice? You need a willingness to do what you are asked to do. How can you have that? Deny yourself. As long as I am full of myself, believe me, I do not want people telling me what to do. That is thoroughly human, thoroughly natural, and quite unspiritual. That is not of the Lord. One of the basic aspects of a person who believes in the Lord Jesus Christ is that so far as his personal, physical, human nature is concerned, it is being yielded and reckoned as if dead. If anyone wants to advise him, the Christian's only question is, does he know what he's talking about? If that person has been over the road, he knows more. That is the person who can help.

Let us look at the phrase, "How thou oughtest to behave thyself." Can you picture what that really means? It means take yourself by the handles as if you were a lawnmower. Take yourself by the handles, point yourself in the right direction, and push yourself in that direction; shove yourself in that direction.

"The house of God" is not a building. We commonly use it as if it were, and we know what we mean. We appreciate the fact that the building is made sacred by usage, but that is not what Paul means by "the house of God." The house of God are the people, not just any people, but those people in whom God dwells.

I think it would make such a difference to us all if, when we go to church services, we would have in mind that this is a company of people in whom God is working. A congregation is very much like a floral display. Out there in your community flowers are growing by the grace of God. Here is a believer, there is an interested person. Your local congregation is made up just as if someone had gone out into the community and picked the flowers. We then expect the pastor and the others to arrange the flowers and set them out, those who have been called out by the living God. By the way, this is one of the few places where the word "church" is used in this way.

> Which is the church of the living God, the pillar and ground of the truth (1 Tim. 3:15).

The word "pillar" is the support under a house that holds up the floor. That is the basis of the truth of God in Christ.

> And without controversy great is the mystery of godliness (1 Tim. 3:16).

Then Paul gives this package description: Timothy was to be an example, in his own conduct, of being godly. What does it mean to be godly? Godliness is the quality of action which shows the reality of God and of His ways of dealing. When a person is living as a believer, something about his reverence towards God, his respect to those in authority, his consideration of other people, his charity to the poor, causes you to say, "That person acts as if he believes." How do you know? Why did he act that way? He did not act that way primarily to imitate anybody, but because of what he believed.

"Manifest in the flesh" makes you think of the incarnation. The Word was made flesh. "Justified in the Spirit" means that He was kept in the will of God by the Spirit of God who filled Him. "Seen of angels" recalls to us that while Jesus of Nazareth was here in this world He was in personal contact with invisible beings. The Gospel was "preached unto the Gentiles," those who did not know God and did not know His Word. "Believed on in the world" brings to our minds the testimony of other believers, all those who believe in the Lord Jesus Christ. "Received up into glory" is where He is now. This whole package of truth can be in the consciousness of any person who believes, and the consciousness of this truth will affect that person and will lead him in ways which will be pleasing to God.

Chapter 16

SOME DOCTRINES SHOULD BE REJECTED

Can you understand that if I tolerate every interpretation of the Bible I am failing to do my duty?

> Now the Spirit speaketh expressly, that in the latter times some shall depart from the faith, giving heed to seducing spirits, and doctrines of devils; speaking lies in hypocrisy; having their conscience seared with a hot iron; forbidding to marry, and commanding to abstain from meats, which God hath created to be received with thanksgiving of them which believe and know the truth (1 Tim. 4:1-3).

The way a man thinks is the basis of his conduct: "As a man thinketh in his heart, so is he." Then how can we consider what a man thinks? How would we know? We know by listening to him, by hearing what he says: "Out of the fullness of the heart the mouth speaketh." Now let us see more in detail what this passage means.

"The Spirit speaketh expressly" means that the Holy Spirit in the hearts of the believers conveys to them exactly the message in these verses. "Expressly" means clearly, plainly stated in obvious terms. How would the Spirit speak expressly? Does that mean that everybody will hear a voice? Does that mean that we will hear words coming out of the air? I would expect this question to come up while praying, because that is when the Spirit is particularly operative. When people gather to pray, the Spirit Himself prays with them, and they feel inwardly led to certain ideas toward God.

"The Spirit speaketh expressly . . . in the latter times." When it comes to thinking of the latter times, there are different views. I have no disposition just now to approve one view or to disapprove another. I have no desire to identify the latter times as any certain stage in the history of the world, or to specify how much time is to be included in any such phase. I know that some do, but I want to be excused from passing judgment on them. However, I want to propose to you that the latter times in the New Testament, may refer to that period of history since Pentecost and until Christ's return, or from the time the Lord Jesus Christ sent the Holy Spirit to dwell in the hearts of people until the day that He appears in the clouds of heaven with ten thousand of His angels.

Certain things are predicted that will occur in the latter times, and you do not need to know very much history to realize that those conditions, events, and happenings, have been going on since the early church until this present day. I know there will be persecution of believers; it has always been that way. I know there will be opposition to the Gospel; it has always been that way. I know there will be signs in nature, earthquakes and storms and pestilence in divers places; that has been going on all the time. I know there will be wars and rumors of wars; I do not know how many wars are going on in the world right now. I think all of these conditions are indicative of latter times.

I am not dating it, though I am bounding it, in what I would consider to be the latter times. Paul says here that in the latter times some shall depart from the faith. Now in this epistle of First Timothy there is a warning note. Go through First Timothy and underscore the word "some." Some people from inside the group of believers have turned away from the truth. Let us not overlook this sober possibility. I should not miss the fact that I could be turned off. I could be lured away. Someone might say to me, "You don't mean that a believer could be deluded?" Yes, that is what I mean to say.

Notice who such are, "Giving heed to seducing spirits." In our day many people have become conscious of the invisible world, and they speak a great deal of spirits of various kinds. Some of these spirits are seducing spirits that would lead a person away from the things of God. They are dangerous, and they are all around us right now. No human being knows enough to escape them. Our only hope is in the Lord. We can put our trust in the Lord Jesus Christ and turn to Him. He is a strong Tower, and we are safe in Him.

"Giving heed to seducing spirits, and doctrines of devils"

Some Doctrines Should Be Rejected

speaks of demons. You might remember the incident in the Garden of Eden when Satan came to speak to Eve. He stated as true certain things that were not true. That was his way of teaching his doctrines. "You shall not surely die," he said. He was wrong. More than that, he was a liar. They would die, and history has proven that they did die. Yet Satan said to Eve, "You shall not surely die."

"Doctrines of devils; speaking lies in hypocrisy" means the Gospel can be discussed insincerely. This means that a person can use all the right words, and produce the wrong idea. The Bible is very plain about this.

"Having their conscience seared with a hot iron" means the conscience can be scorched or made callous, insensitive. Paul spoke earlier in this letter to Timothy about some people who with reference to their faith had turned away from conscience. Here there are people talking about the Gospel whose conscience has been seared, hardened; as if it were with a scar of burning over it.

"Forbidding to marry, and commanding to abstain from meats, which God hath created to be received with thanksgiving of them which believe and know the truth." Some people say such things even though the Scriptures do not teach this. Paul then referred to certain things that he could foresee would come to pass. So far as you and I are concerned we are being warned with this one big general idea: you cannot believe everybody. As a matter of fact, if it comes from mere human beings you cannot believe anything. You should look up, take the Word of God in your hand and in your heart, read it, and believe God. Your life depends upon it. Your salvation depends upon it. Eternal life depends upon it. Believe God and no one else.

Chapter 17

GOOD DOCTRINE SHOULD BE PREACHED

In a world of turmoil and confusion, is it possible for anybody to live a quiet and peaceable life?

> For every creature of God is good, and nothing to be refused, if it be received with thanksgiving: for it is sanctified by the word of God and prayer. If thou put the brethren in remembrance of these things, thou shalt be a good minister of Jesus Christ, nourished up in the words of faith and of good doctrine, whereunto thou hast attained (1 Tim. 4:4-6).

Rules and regulations designed to lead people into blessing are important. The reason for them is our natural lack of desire, lack of interest, lack of intention in our natural hearts to do the right thing. In all sincerity man can consider some natural practices to be evil when actually there is no evil present. In directing a believer's mode of living no such artificial regulations are in order. Rules can be helpful to the natural man, but they are not involved in the life of faith. Nobody has to tell the sun to shine, and nobody has to tell the water to be wet. That is just the way it is. All things as created by God are good when they are taken as they are made. This may seem astonishing to some, but it is true. Let me repeat this point.

> I know, and am persuaded by the Lord Jesus, that there is nothing unclean of itself: but to him that esteemeth any thing to be unclean, to him it is unclean (Rom. 14:14).

This is an insight that needs to be learned from the Word of God. It is never so much the thing in itself that is wrong, it is the situation in which it occurs. Consider a simple illustration: eating an apple is not wrong, but for me to eat your apple against your wishes is wrong. The quality of an action is not so much derived from the action in itself, it is derived from the relationship which is involved. This is not only true of material things, but this is true of pleasures, of fellowships, of opportunities, of anything that is provided by God in His providence before us. It is to be received with thanksgiving. When I am in any given situation, whether it may seem good or bad, my heart is to be aware of the fact this is from God. To Him be the glory!

Notice that all things need to be sanctified. What does the word "sanctified" mean? It means "set apart unto God." "By the word of God" means by the revealed will of God. If a person wants to know what the revealed will of God is, he will study the Bible. A person can read it there. "And prayer" means that he has deliberately committed this particular matter to God. This needs to be done.

"If thou put the brethren in remembrance of these things," or said another way, "If in your preaching, you will remind your people of this," what does that imply? It means that the truth about any given matter is not implicit. The action in itself will never show the evil in it. This will be seen in the situation in which it occurs. It is not from the natural processes that you will learn this. You must be told. There must be teaching. There must be revelation.

If Timothy put the brethren in remembrance of these things, "thou shalt be a good minister of Jesus Christ." A minister of Jesus Christ is one who shares Jesus Christ: he is one who brings Jesus Christ to the people. He is the waiter at the restaurant who brings in your food. The minister brings to the people the truth for their good. Anybody, whether he is a minister, a Sunday school teacher, a mother, a father, a friend, a neighbor, who is a witness for Jesus Christ should help all other believers to remember that the real truth of things is seen in their spiritual significance.

Paul goes on to say, "nourished up in the words of faith and of good doctrine." It appears that faith needs to be fed. Faith is not something that I can do in myself, whenever I may want to do it. "Faith cometh by hearing and hearing by the Word of God." Faith needs to be built in a person by words of good doctrine. Not all doctrine is good. Any number of people who are talking about the Gospel are not telling the truth. The soul needs to be fed with the words of faith and of good doctrine.

Faith and trust in God are to be nurtured by the Bible, the Word of God, which is milk to the new believer and meat to the experienced, mature believer. In the words of faith the Scriptures reveal the invisible God to the soul: they show the plan of God according to the promises and good doctrine. Not all interpretation of Scripture is good. To be good for a person, the interpretation must be true to what is actually revealed from God. It is sad but true that deception about the Gospel is possible. Denaturing the Gospel is possible. The truth about the Lord Jesus Christ can be twisted. No wonder that the Lord Himself says, "Take heed that no man deceive you."

I will now mention something for you if you are a Bible student; this will be an idea for you to notice. In the New Testament there are a number of "second" epistles: Second Corinthians, Second Thessalonians, Second Timothy, Second Peter, and Second John. I would not make a dogmatic statement about this, but you can check it out. Each one of these warns against possible error. The first epistle in each case tells some great truth, and the second epistle warns against being fooled. This whole matter of coming to believe in God through the Lord Jesus Christ is a matter of understanding what the Bible teaches, and then feeding the soul on that.

Chapter 18

GODLINESS IS VERY IMPORTANT

Can you understand why a believer should promote his own faith in serving the Lord?

As Paul is instructing Timothy, so that Timothy in turn might guide believers into fruitful and blessed living, Paul makes a great point of personal application of the truth to Timothy himself.

> But refuse profane and old wives' fables, and exercise thyself rather unto godliness. For bodily exercise profiteth little: but godliness is profitable unto all things, having promise of the life that now is, and of that which is to come. This is a faithful saying and worthy of all acceptation. For therefore we both labour and suffer reproach, because we trust in the living God, who is the Saviour of all men, specially of those that believe. These things command and teach (1 Tim. 4:7-11).

There are precautions that any minister should take about himself. Any preacher should be careful about his own frame of mind. Any witness for the Lord should take care about himself as he stands up before the world. Any believer, so far as his testimony is concerned, should be careful about the image he presents to the world about him. Apparently a minister, and that is what Timothy was, should guard his menu and supervise his diet. He should not expose himself to everything.

Some years ago it was my privilege to go to a certain student convention in Chicago. I heard a man speaking to those students, and I was impressed by the short message that he gave. He told about himself in words like this: "I put a watch to guard over my mind. I put the soldiers out there at the gate. I challenge everything that enters into my mind. And the way I do that is when I pick up a book to read it, I am against it. I read all things with antipathy until they are proven to be acceptable." I remember how stirred I was because I felt how wise and sound that is.

Any person who is wise will be careful about his food. Tainted food must be avoided. If that is true physically, it is just as true mentally and morally and spiritually. There is a popular notion today that you should taste everything. That notion is not valid. It is not good. Ideas come to your mind with a reputation. Ideas have an image about them. The humble, committed believer simply is not open to entertain every passing notion.

The believer has been retained by the Lord. He is betrothed to his Lord and Savior as a bride is to her bridegroom. He is an enlisted service man. He has signed up. The believer is on duty at all times. He is living in a world that is at war. There is an enemy, and he must not let that enemy get inside his own mind and heart. There are diseases that are dangerous, and if he is to stay healthy and well, he must take precautions. If that is true physically, that is true spiritually.

Note how Paul writes to Timothy, "Refuse profane and old wives' fables." Paul does not outline their contents. He does not tell what those fables are. In all Paul's writing, he never publicizes error by describing it so that he can refute it or refer to it. There are old wives' fables, profane ideas that bring down the truth of the Gospel, false notions around that actually enter the image of the Scripture, that is true. Avoid them. That is all Paul says.

"Exercise thyself rather unto godliness." Have you ever gone through a system of exercises to keep yourself in health? If you have you will know what this means. You must take yourself in hand to perform those exercises. You might do them a time or two for curiosity, but sooner or later this gets old. Godliness is never casual. You cannot just be godly in any easy fashion. It is not done by simply allowing things to happen with the hope that then you will be godly.

Such blessing is never casual; and such blessing is never unrelated to what you do. As a matter of fact, it is a consequence. It is to be achieved by an intelligent effort. There are things you can do that will promote godliness. Godliness has elements of behavior that result from faith in God. If you exercise yourself in this way you will exercise your faith in God.

Godliness Is Very Important

Let us consider what Paul points out, because he describes it. He goes on to say, "For bodily exercise profiteth little." The language of the text seems to yield itself to the translation that bodily exercise does profit a little. Paul does not say there is anything wrong with physical exercise; but he would say it has a limited value. It helps only a little, because even if by exercise you were to have a body that is physically perfect, so what? The body is still limited in its time of being on earth. Threescore years, or maybe fourscore years, just a short time and soon it will be gone.

"But godliness is profitable unto all things, having promise of the life that now is." You can actually have the life of God in you right now. By believing in the Lord Jesus Christ and committing yourself to Him, you can have the presence of God in your soul right now. When you leave this world you will go into the presence of God, and the same Lord who was with you here will be with you there. "This is a faithful saying and worthy of all acceptation." Living with God in heaven and actually looking forward to being with Him is a worthy thing; it is worthy of all acceptation. You can afford to put it at the top of your list.

"For therefore we both labor and suffer reproach." Paul's life in the ministry was not an easy one. "Because we trust in the living God," so his actions were often different from those of other people. They trust in other men, they trust in themselves, they work out things the best they know how; but the believer trusts in the living God who is the Savior of all men. This is a matter that will cause some thought. In what sense can you honestly say that God is the Savior of all men? Does this mean that all men will have eternal life? No; other Scripture helps us here:

> Enter ye in at the strait gate: for wide is the gate, and broad is the way, that leadeth to destruction, and many there be which go in thereat: because strait is the gate, and narrow is the way, which leadeth unto life, and few there be that find it (Matt. 7:13-14).

Then what do you mean when you say He is the Savior of all men? I think it means that He came willing to save all men. He gave Himself for all men and died for them.

Many people will not receive Him; they ignore Him, and despise Him. But He died for them just the same. I think the word "saved" does not always refer only to eternal life, in the sense that you are going to be with God and not go to hell. It has that in it, but that is not all that is in it. I think that being saved also means that day in and day out you have the blessing of God as you live. God Himself will lift you and carry you along with Himself.

Then Paul ends this admonition by saying to Timothy, "These things command and teach." What does that imply? He might have said, "What I have been talking about is not the natural way for people to act. Ordinarily they would not accept it. I want you to direct the believers to live this way, and teach it to them. Show them how it will be. It is not the natural way, but it is the spiritual way. It is God's way, and it is the way of blessing."

Chapter 19

THE MINISTER OF THE GOSPEL SHOULD BE AN EXAMPLE

Can you see how a believer, young in years, could be an inspiring example to others?

The life of any group of people is inspired and directed by their accepted leaders. The leader acts in the name of the people, on account of the people, and for the sake of the people. If he is a true leader, he recognizes that his function is to put into action what the people themselves want to have put into action. His public image is the preferred image for the people. While the leader may not be able to dictate the exact image, he does have a lot of influence in what people will be expecting and thinking.

Paul wanted Timothy to do what was necessary to boost his own image before the eyes of the people. Paul knew that Timothy was a young minister, dealing with a group of people, many of whom were older than Timothy. They had been through hard experiences in the Gospel, and he was to preach the Gospel to them. In order that he might do that effectively, it was essential that they think well of him.

> Let no man despise thy youth; but be thou an example of the believers, in word, in conversation, in charity, in spirit, in faith, in purity. Till I come, give attendance to reading, to exhortation, to doctrine. Neglect not the gift that is in thee, which was given thee by prophecy, with the laying on of the hands of the presbytery (1 Tim. 4:12-14).

"Let no man despise thy youth." Why was this important? If anyone who looks youthful attempts to lead, people will be inclined to say about him, "Why, he is just a boy!" When that has been said, there may be appreciation for him personally, and there may be a willingness to accept his personal testimony, but some will question the need to follow his judgment. How could a young man overcome the popular notion that if he is young he will not amount to much? He could do this by the way he acted. People generally think a young man is overly enthusiastic, even flighty perhaps, lacking good judgment. But if Timothy acted gravely, soberly, cautiously, under control; if he did not get overly enthusiastic about anything, was not easily discouraged, was steadfast, people would say about him, "He may be young, but he has an old head on those young shoulders of his." People will get the impression that he is a reliable person.

Then there follows a description of the things that Timothy should do that he might accomplish this end. "Be thou an example of the believers." This young minister was to be an example to the other believers. Paul suggests several different ways in which he could do this, such as, "in word." I think this means far more than just language. I think this includes how he handles the Bible. If he is to be an example "in word," the idea of the Word of God is not far away. He was to be very careful in the way he talked. "In conversation": conversation means much more than just talk. Conversation implies the manner of life. That is what is in the Greek. "In his manner of life" would mean that when people saw how he lived they would know that he was not a novice. They would know that he was a solid citizen if he were careful in his speech.

"In charity" would be another very real indication of maturity. Charity is shown when you exercise yourself on behalf of the poor. Your concern for their welfare is noticeable, and this contributes to your image. "In spirit" means to say in your attitude, in your purpose, in your interest in things, you will manifest the fact that you really are a true believer. How would "in faith" show up? When anything happened that would involve a question of confidence in God, and one would wonder what to do, Timothy was to manifest his faith in God by choosing to do it God's way even though the circumstances were against him. People would soon recognize his example and would come to realize that he was a true believer. "In purity" has to do with morality, but I think it is more than that. I think that this matter of purity would have in it the idea of unselfishness, of being absolutely a totally dedicated person.

The Minister of the Gospel Should Be an Example

So in all these, in word, in conversation, in charity, in spirit, in faith, in purity Timothy was to be an example. He was to live it out in the open.

How could he live it before people? "Till I come, give attendance to reading, to exhortation, to doctrine." These three activities promote the very thing that Paul wanted Timothy to have. Of course, reading the sacred writing would be major. I am not sure it would be limited to that, but I am sure it would have in it the idea of Timothy's getting in touch with the minds of other men to see what serious-minded people had written. Exhortation is urging other people to live the right way. When he would be interested in how other people were doing and seeking to win them to the Lord, this would be noticeable. Doctrine would refer to his teaching, the explanation of doctrine and getting this across to people. This is how his witness could be given.

"Neglect not the gift that is in thee, which was given thee by prophecy, with the laying on of the hands of the presbytery." Now this is a verse that is not very clear for us in our day and time. We do not have many instances that are like this verse, because I am afraid that we do not make use of much of this. Prophecy I understand to be the exercise of interpreting Scripture and has to do with preaching. The gift is divine enablement. The gift would be something that would be given to Timothy that would enable him to accomplish things for the Lord. This capacity to do things for the Lord was in Timothy because of the preaching that had been done before him. I am inclined to think that the laying on of the hands of the presbytery implies the idea that the older men, the elders, who constitute the presbytery, certified Timothy for service. They instructed him to go ahead and do certain things. They ordained him. They committed themselves to support him. This would be a real challenge to Timothy and would draw him out.

Paul wanted Timothy to remember that the church as a whole trusted him, and gave him the privilege of preaching. Paul said, "Neglect not." How do you "neglect not"? Use it. This gift has been given to you for service. You do not have it just to enjoy it. You do not have it just to be able to think that you are better than other people. You should use the insights you now have into the will of God. Timothy was a young man who had been called into the ministry. Older men had certified him to Paul and encouraged Paul to take him along as his servant. Then they had instructed Timothy from the Scriptures as to what the will of God was for him. All of that gave Timothy a certain fitness to serve, so that he had an inward divine enablement to serve.

It was a gift that he should use to the glory of God.

Chapter 20

THE MINISTER IS RESPONSIBLE

Can you understand how the spiritual life of the preacher has a direct bearing on the life of his hearers?

> Meditate upon these things; give thyself wholly to them; that thy profiting may appear to all. Take heed unto thyself, and unto the doctrine; continue in them: for in doing this thou shalt both save thyself, and them that hear thee (1 Tim. 4:15-16).

Paul wanted Timothy to be effective; we would say, to be successful. He knew there was only one way to be effective, and that would be to go the way of the cross. This needs close consideration. Walking in the way of the cross is not an easy thing. A good many people may feel that yielding to the Lord Jesus Christ, and then walking in the way of the cross, is a sort of resignation from activity, or taking the easy way out. Those people have never done it, I can tell you that. They have never tried it, because the way of the cross will involve you just as it involved Jesus of Nazareth. Living your life for Christ is not easy.

We do read that the Lord, for the joy that was set before Him, endured the cross, despising the shame, and is now set down at the right hand of God. We are told to look to Him and take Him as our leader and follow Him. This is what Paul wanted Timothy to do. In this passage Paul leads Timothy to feel his responsibility. This is something for us all to learn. The believer has a responsibility to prepare to walk by faith. When a believer is in his home as the husband and father, he is trusting in the Lord Jesus Christ. The Lord wants the man's personal effect upon his family to be wholesome. We should note that for the believer this is not going to be easy. There is something that he needs to do every day as he goes along, and this will challenge everything that is in him.

Denying oneself is not easy. Paul wanted Timothy to prepare himself, because he wanted Timothy to be able to do that by which the people would be blessed. How should a preacher prepare himself that he might minister in faith? As we are thinking about the minister we could also think of a family. What should a mother do? What should a father do? What should a brother do? What should a sister do? What should you do among your friends? If you believe in the Lord Jesus Christ, and you would like to be helpful in ministering to other people, how could you get yourself ready?

Let us note what Paul tells Timothy to do. The first thing he should do is to "meditate upon these things." He is to think about what Paul is telling him. He is to turn these things over in his mind. He is to contemplate what the promises are, and look at what the warnings are. What are these "things?" He should meditate on the things of Christ. What would that be? Christ Jesus came to seek and to save the lost; Timothy should think about that. Was he one of the lost? Then Christ came for him. Christ Jesus bore away his sins, reconciling him to God. Any person expecting to minister today should think about that. He should meditate on that. Every day will not be perfect for him. He will not always do everything that he should do.

Furthermore, the minister should meditate upon this, that Christ will carry away his sins. Christ bears away all the sins of the minister. The blood of the Lord Jesus Christ cleanseth him from every stain. If he should say, "What will I do?" he will know what to do. He will thank the Lord, and he will praise Him. But more is true in the Gospel than that. Christ arose from the dead. He is alive now. The believer should think about this. He is interceding for us. He is praying for you. He is praying for me. He is praying for every believer. And He is coming again. The world will see Him. You and I are going to Him. The glorious part is yet to come. "Meditate upon these things; give thyself wholly to them." These words sound simple. But we need to bring our whole attention to it. We should focus all our consciousness on these things that I have been discussing.

"That thy profiting may appear to all," because just as surely as you will meditate upon these things briefly outlined here, you will profit thereby. How? Your faith will grow greater, and it will expand in its understanding. As your faith grows, you will remember more and more of the truth, and believe more and more of the truth. This will show up in your conduct. Everybody will see it. You will have love toward God and toward man. You will have joy in the Lord. You will have peace in your own soul. These things will show up. The fruits of the Spirit will be there, and other people will see them. You are the one who is gaining thereby, but other people will see these things and be strengthened.

Paul went on to write: "Take heed unto thyself." Be careful what you do. What did he mean by that? I can imagine somebody might say: "I am not going to steal anything. I am not going to break anything." Wait a minute. There's more. You should be careful in what you do. What do you read? To what do you give your mind? What do you talk about with people? What do you look at when you have your choice? What do you say? What do you think? Now these are all things that you do. Watch yourself, brother.

"And unto the doctrine" means you are to take heed unto the doctrine. You cannot change it. You are not going to improve it, and you are not going to cut it down in any other way. It will be there in the Scriptures when you are through with it. But how can you take heed unto it? By remembering what the Bible says. It is not just what you think. It is not just the way you have it figured. It is what the Bible says. This is the doctrine.

"Continue in them." This brings up a very important idea. I wonder how much I can make clear. You do not only read and study that you may understand. You do not only bring it all together so that you can know it. You do not only go through the experience of being greatly blessed. But you continue in the promises of God, and God will redeem you. He will redeem you regardless of what you do. He knew about you when Christ Jesus died for you; and Christ Jesus died for you to redeem you from all sin while you were yet a sinner. God will have fellowship with you. He is sending His Holy Spirit to be with you. He wants to be with you, so continue in that. God will answer your prayer. God will guide you. God will keep you. God will bless you. God will forgive you. God will cleanse you. I could go on and on, but I want to tell you what I am emphasizing: you and I are to continue in these things. Keep them before us at all times.

Now listen to this. "In doing this thou shalt both save thyself, and them that hear thee." Someone could say right away, "Well, only the Lord can save me." I know, but you can take hold of His hand. You can look in His direction. Just as surely as you look to Him, He will look to you. Such action and behavior as I have briefly outlined here will bring blessing to you and will save you. You will be personally blessed in your own soul, forgiven, cleansed, comforted, made joyful, glad, and you will bring all who hear you into this kind of blessedness. Never forget the promise is to you and to your children.

Chapter 21

PRACTICAL GUIDANCE FOR GODLY CONDUCT

If a person's heart is right with God, would he profit by having instructions on how to act?

As we read along in Paul's instructions to Timothy, we find that Paul was very specific about certain advice that he gave to Timothy. As I read this, I ask myself, if Timothy needed this advice, would not I or any of us need the same?

> Rebuke not an elder, but entreat him as a father; and the younger men as brethren; the elder women as mothers; the younger as sisters, with all purity. Honour widows that are widows indeed. But if any widow have children or nephews, let them learn first to show piety at home, and to requite their parents: for that is good and acceptable before God (1 Tim. 5:1-4).

We find here that Paul urges Timothy to deal with other believers as he would deal with members of his own family. When we look at these words: "Rebuke not an elder," that is fairly clear. You can understand what that means if you say to yourself, "Do not sharply censure an older person or rebuke an older man." I am sure the word "elder" possibly refers to a person who has a certain office in the church or the congregation, but it may not be an official title. It may be just descriptive of an older person. In other words, do not act as if you were the boss or as if you were the inspector.

But suppose that older person is not right but is at fault? Then Paul goes on to say you are to treat him as a father. What would that mean? Respect him and spare his feelings. Some years ago I picked up these lines and they have lingered in my memory through the years: "Speak gently to the aged one, grieve not the careworn heart. The sands of life are nearly run, let such in peace depart." I think that is a fine word. The person who is inwardly trusting in God, resting in God, being inwardly moved by the Holy Spirit of God, will find that this will suit his inward feelings and that his attitude toward older people will be one of respect and of carefulness. Go easy with them if they are older.

By the way, in being realistic about this, it is not always easy to act this way. I can tell you that sometimes these older people are the most unreasonable persons you ever saw. I am reminded that George Mueller, a great man of faith whose name is well-known among all people who are interested in prayer life, recorded in his diary a prayer of his: "God keep me from ever being a wicked old man." In case a person reading this is older, let me commend it to you. Be very careful that you humble yourself before God. But Paul is talking to the younger people and saying regardless of how that older person acts, treat him with respect. I am saying it means speak gently to the aged ones.

Paul goes on to say, ". . . the younger men as brethren," that is to say, those of your own age group. How would you treat a person as a brother? Treat him not merely with courtesy but with concern. You are interested in him, and you are concerned about the things that concern him. You want his welfare; you want his joy; you want him to have fellowship and communion with others. By the way, we can have in mind that this would be equally true among younger women—that all believing women should treat each other as sisters. Normally speaking this would mean that a brother in his actions toward his sister would certainly work for and act for her protection. He would be interested in her companionship and in her blessing.

Paul goes on, "Honor widows that are widows indeed." The word "widow" as it is used in the Greek may mean a woman or a man. There is no such word in the Greek as "widower." The word refers simply to those who are left alone and, generally speaking, left destitute. So when you say "honor widows that are widows indeed," Paul is saying be concerned for the poor, those that have no friends, the lonely ones. But take note of their circumstances. Not every one of them actually needs your help. Do not let anybody exploit you and take advantage of you. Would some do that? Yes, they would. But if they were

Practical Guidance For Godly Conduct

believers and were in the church, would they take advantage of you? Yes, I am sorry to say they might. They are still human beings. So you should be careful not to give your kindness and mercy in every direction. You have a responsibility to check the circumstances and be sure your generosity is proper.

"But if any widow have children or nephews, let them learn first to show piety at home, and to requite their parents." Members of the family who can care for those who are unable to care for themselves are to learn first to show piety at home. How would you show piety? Act in such a manner as to please God by respecting those in authority, by consideration of others, and by showing charity to the poor. "Honor thy father and mother." In that way you would be showing piety, and you should do it at home. Family relationships are more basic than social affairs. The old, well-known saying is so true, "Charity begins at home."

Chapter 22

HONEST RESPONSIBILITY IS ESSENTIAL

Can you understand that what a person does makes all the difference in how he is to be esteemed?

> Now she that is a widow indeed, and desolate, trusteth in God, and continueth in supplications and prayers night and day. But she that liveth in pleasure is dead while she liveth. And these things give in charge, that they may be blameless. But if any provide not for his own, and specially for those of his own house, he hath denied the faith, and is worse than an infidel (1 Tim. 5:5-8).

It is a common failing among human beings that a person will say one thing and then do another. On account of that we have learned to say: "Talk is cheap," and "Actions speak louder than words." We may feel some surprise that Paul, writing to a church leader like Timothy, should bring up for emphasis such simple matters as he does. But there is profound truth here. Walking in the will of God is not a matter of some specific action. It is not some peculiar or extraordinary thing that you do. Walking in the will of God takes place while you are doing your daily routine. The actions of any person are largely shaped by his circumstances, structured by the situation in which he lives, largely determined by others; but how I am doing it is my personal responsibility. For this I am judged, and in this I can be helped by God.

The words of this Scripture we have read are found in a discussion that Paul has set down for Timothy. Paul pointed out how Timothy should act with people as he applies the Word to them. Paul emphasizes here the principle of family responsibility. This principle is particularly applied to taking care of the needy in the family, but the principle is true in every case. Paul shows how it is involved with believers. In writing to Timothy he is writing largely with reference to the people whom the world would call Christian; but it is a truth for everybody. It is always true when God sets people in families that the family is a structure of fellowship and responsibility. Everyone in the family belongs to everyone else in that family. Each member has something to share with each other and something to do for each other. Paul pointed out to Timothy that as pastor, when he was going on to teach people and show them especially what would be acceptable to God, he should remember that it is the way they act that really counts.

Let us look at these words more closely: "Now she that is a widow indeed." This is simply a person who is desolate or alone. "She that is a widow indeed, and desolate, trusteth in God, and continueth in supplications and prayers night and day." I do not think that means that she is on her knees all the time with her eyes shut and her hands folded in prayer; but she is constantly in that frame of mind. She is trusting in God, and as far as she is concerned she is living in dependence upon God.

Does such a person always get immediate answers? No. Then what is the point in praying? Far more is involved in praying than simply getting something. Prayer begins with coming to God, putting one's trust in God, and fellowshiping with God. Often prayer is an occasion when the individual can unburden his heart to God. What happens when a person prays continually? Such a person gains assurance that "God will"; and "He will." A person who is in a frame of mind to pray to God always gains understanding that God has "done" for him; God is "doing" for him; God will "do" for him. By the time a person reviews all that, he can say to his heart, "What are you worried about?"

Praying to God is not merely an easy way to get benefits from God. It is not as though somehow in the presence of God all His possible benefits for us were set out in some sort of smorgasbord, so we could go up and select what we want. Praying to God is not a matter of telling God what to do. God knows everything, and He knows what He will do. Praying to God is committing oneself to God. It is a matter of asking for help. It is asking for blessing. It is bringing our problems to God. Actually the believer is strengthened to know that the greatest blessing he could have is that God's will should be done. There is one thing the believer can keep in mind with joy: God is minded to do good to him; God is benevolent; He is kind; He is gracious. The person who waits continuously before God is reminded of that regardless of the circumstances.

Now in this particular instance Paul is discussing a person who is alone, a widow. When she turns to God and clings to God she is blessed. Then Paul goes on to say, "But she that liveth in pleasure is dead while she liveth." "Pleasure" is doing what she wants to do. Though this is being discussed with reference to women, this is true also with reference to men. The point is that the person who lives in this world; who acts in line with his own personal desires, his own wishes, his own pleasure, is dead. This means to say he is unresponsive to God even though he seems to be alive. As far as living is concerned, we are not always on a picnic. Sometimes in the course of living, our actions are selfish and indulgent, and sometimes we are tempted to be spiteful or moved to envy, and all of this would be along the line of living in pleasure. This is doing as we like to do and as we want to do. When that is true, that soul is not responsive to God.

> But if any provide not for his own, and specially for those of his own house, he hath denied the faith, and is worse than an infidel (1 Tim. 5:8).

What does this mean? This refers to a person who has not responded to the guidance of the Holy Spirit of God. If a person has come to God, has yielded himself to God, God has given him the Holy Spirit of God within him. He cannot feel God, hear Him, touch Him, but he can believe Him. If a person does not provide for his own, so that he takes care of his own family, he is denying that inward guidance of the Lord. Such a person, Paul says, is worse than an infidel. Why would he say this? Apparently the infidel would be ignorant, but this person Paul is talking about is not ignorant. He knows what the Lord would have him do, but he is not doing it. We conclude that it matters to God how we handle our practical affairs.

Chapter 23

THE UNWORTHY SHOULD NOT RECEIVE CHARITY BENEFITS

Do you realize that a preacher is responsible for care in endorsing someone?

Isn't it true that people feel a preacher should accept anybody regardless of how he lives or what he does? Will it shock you if I say that this is not the way it should be in all cases? To be entitled to support from a congregation (and the minister represents the congregation), a person should qualify as being reliable, with a good record. I would like to emphasize that God will receive anybody who will come; however, that does not mean that the preacher is to endorse by his approval anybody who shows up.

Let us look in this passage for the principle that is involved:

> Let not a widow be taken into the number under threescore years old, having been the wife of one man, well reported of for good works; if she have brought up children, if she have lodged strangers, if she have washed the saints' feet, if she have relieved the afflicted, if she have diligently followed every good work. But the younger widows refuse: for when they have begun to wax wanton against Christ, they will marry; having damnation, because they have cast off their first faith. And withal they learn to be idle, wandering about from house to house; and not only idle, but tattlers also and busybodies, speaking things which they ought not (1 Tim. 5:9-13).

"Let not a widow be taken into the number under threescore years old, having been the wife of one man." Because the preacher is acting for the whole congregation, he must be careful what he decides to do and with whom he is going to deal. When you use the word "widow" you will remember you mean any bereft person, without relatives, or a person without money. The word can refer to either a man or a woman. Now to be eligible for support from the church, here is the point, such a person must have a good report. It is interesting to notice that Paul would have the person be at least sixty years of age and with a good record, "well reported of for good works."

Then Paul outlines what those good works should be. "If she have brought up children, if she have lodged strangers (she would extend the hospitality of her home to strangers), if she have washed the saints' feet." You and I may not know much about that, but it means that she has been willing to do the work of a humble servant. Washing the feet of a visitor was done by a humble servant. Such a woman has been willing to be humble. "If she have relieved the afflicted," she has been charitable. "If she have diligently followed every good work. . . ." I do not know a better word to use than "pious." That is a good word even though oftentimes it has been discounted, perhaps because so many people have pretended a piety that they did not have. But there is nothing wrong with being a pious person. The church was to be charitable toward that kind of person.

"Well reported of for good works" would raise a question in the minds of many people. Are not we supposed to help anyone in need? Yes, but Paul would say, "Be very careful in this." The example of the Good Samaritan is applicable in any case. We are to do good to others from the standpoint of helping the man who is in dire need. That is a special situation; but what Paul is referring to here is the matter of taking on a certain continuing responsibility.

Paul told Timothy to be very careful not to use the church's money indiscriminately: not to give it out just to everybody and everywhere. Paul urges Timothy to see that the church evaluate the candidate for the church's benevolence. This seems to mean that only the worthy church members are eligible for the church's support. Unworthy people should not impose upon the charity of the church. We are inclined to think there should be no judgment of the people we help. It has been such common practice that we feel anybody at all is eligible for the goodness of God. If that is true, we ought to be good and kind to everybody. But here Paul told Timothy, "Be very careful how you use the generosity of the church."

I know there are Scriptures that make you think there is no

The Unworthy Should Not Receive Charity Benefits

question about what kind of person should receive the blessing of God. For instance, "God is no respecter of persons," which is wonderfully true; and "Whosoever will may come" is also wonderfully true. But these passages can be abused. These Scriptures refer to the door that is open to the grace of God for the salvation of the soul. But does this mean that anybody can come to the church and ask for brotherly help when he is not a brother? Is Paul saying that charitable help is to be withheld from anyone who is deemed unfit? It would seem so. Therefore, notice how this places emphasis on the kind of person with whom you are dealing.

"But the younger widows refuse: for when they have begun to wax wanton against Christ, they will marry; having damnation, because they have cast off their first faith." But is it possible for a person who has been walking with Christ to become wanton; to actually choose another and stay away from Christ? Apparently it is, and apparently this was possible in the congregation. Why does Paul want to avoid putting such people on the roll of dependents? He did not want any enthusiastic believer or congregation to assume responsibilities which might later be discontinued, causing hurt. This is not a simple matter. Paul did not want persons who were receiving benefits to be tempted to drift into careless conduct. With help from the congregation they could afford to be idle and still have enough to live on. Does this imply we must take precautions so that our giving does not encourage idleness? That is just what it means.

Is this a sound principle for family procedures? Is it possible that a parent might do too much for a child? This seems to be possible. It often occurs that the child who grows up under hard circumstances develops into a productive person. While it is sad to say that many times a boy or girl who could have anything he or she wanted at home, is totally unfit to face the world. Such seem to expect that people will give them everything, and that is not true. In this whole passage we are encouraged, in fact we are instructed, to be careful how we act toward others even in charity.

Chapter 24

TREATMENT OF OTHER BELIEVERS SHOULD BE GODLY

Can you understand why a believer should not accept as true any accusation against a leader that comes from only one source?

> I will therefore that the younger women marry, bear children, guide the house, give none occasion to the adversary to speak reproachfully. For some are already turned aside after Satan. If any man or woman that believeth have widows, let them relieve them, and let not the church be charged; that it may relieve them that are widows indeed. Let the elders that rule well be counted worthy of double honor, especially they who labour in the word and doctrine. For the scripture saith, Thou shalt not muzzle the ox that treadeth out the corn. And, The labourer is worthy of his reward. Against an elder receive not an accusation, but before two or three witnesses (1 Tim. 5:14-19).

When Paul instructed Timothy how to conduct himself as a minister, he did not dwell on the contents of the Gospel message. In First Timothy you will not find Paul discussing the doctrines that Timothy was to preach. The letter of Paul to Timothy encourages Timothy to minister the Gospel in daily situations.

This word "minister" takes the truth of the Lord Jesus Christ, the very truth that the believer has in heart and mind, and shows what that should be in daily conduct. For instance, it is an easy thing to say, "Love one another," but now the minister must show people this means not to say anything unkind about anybody. This means that a person will act toward other people the way God acts toward him. That means that even when others are not worthy, he will treat them as the creatures of God. God made them, and God wants to save them, and so the believer wants to win them to God. This will

Treatment of Other Believers Should Be Godly 89

all be in the mind of the believer when he is exercising himself in loving others.

Paul dwelt upon the practical application of Gospel truth. Anyone knowing the Gospel would know that charity is a proper exercise of the believer who knows the grace of Christ. When a person is acting charitably he will be inclined to accept all others as being sincere. However, this might not be realistic, and so Paul urges Timothy as a minister to alert the believers to the fact that not everybody is alike, and not everybody is equally obedient to God.

The words of Jesus of Nazareth are plain. They may shock you. "Give not that which is holy unto the dogs, neither cast ye your pearls before swine" (Matt. 7:6). For a believer to carry out that command he must exercise judgment. It will be necessary to decide who are the swine and who are the dogs. He must make a judgment of motive and an appraisal of the other person's attitude. Who will know how to do that? This is where the minister functions. He is to open the Gospel of the Lord Jesus Christ and show what it means. He must show to the congregation how this judging should be done.

"I will therefore that the younger women marry, bear children, guide the house, give none occasion to the adversary to speak reproachfully. For some are already turned aside after Satan." The social circumstances may vary, but the principle here is that the believers who are younger women are to conduct themselves in a proper fashion. They are to take up a natural way of living, and be careful to act discreetly and above reproach. Thus they will avoid the peril that is mentioned in verse 15: "For some are already turned aside after Satan." There is no mention here of any doctrinal error. They did not turn aside after Satan because they denied that Christ died on the cross, or they denied that He rose from the dead, or they denied that God would receive sinners. They turned aside after Satan in their daily conduct, in their manner of living. They were doing the things that pleased themselves, as Eve did when she ate the fruit. Satan is still tempting, and people are still doing wrong in just that fashion.

"If any man or woman that believeth have widows, let them relieve them, and let not the church be charged; that it may relieve them that are widows indeed." Family responsibility should come first before church responsibility. The congregation as a whole should help the poor; but brothers, sisters, mothers, fathers, and cousins should take first responsibility for helping. If the family would do as they should about their own needy relatives, more would be available to help those who are widows indeed.

Timothy was to teach and to preach and to practice this interpretation. Now this is confusing in our time, because today the civil government does so much charity. People receive help altogether apart from the kind of people they are. As long as their names are on the roll, they receive the money. Because of that, one is inclined to feel the church ought to do the same. But a basic truth is here for believers in Christ. Families should care for their own and not depend upon the congregation to do it; then the congregation can help those who have no family.

"Let the elders that rule well be counted worthy of double honor, especially they who labour in the word and doctrine. For the Scripture saith, 'Thou shalt not muzzle the ox that treadeth out the corn.' And 'The labourer is worthy of his reward.'" Special respect should be shown toward the elders who rule well. Double honor should be given to them. Now do you see how this requires you to exercise some judgment? The conduct of a church officer is known to everybody because it is visible, but not all church officers are equally diligent. Should the congregation then rate their officers? Actually the congregation does this inevitably. Should there be a difference in treatment? It comes naturally, and that difference is proper. Special respect is due to the man who puts in special faithfulness. He is entitled to it.

"Against an elder receive not an accusation, but before two or three witnesses." This is important for the morale of the whole congregation. People will talk; and some people will believe the worst they hear, and will repeat it. Such gossip is injurious to everyone, to the person being talked about and the person who is doing the talking. The elder stands out in front and above, and he is an easy target. Remember that the minister is the teaching elder. Here is a thought for us to have in mind: the leader, the minister, the elder, the preacher, needs protection and deserves protection.

Chapter 25

THE MINISTER MUST JUDGE FAITHFULLY

Can you see that the basic spiritual principle the minister of Christ must use is self-denial?

> Them that sin rebuke before all, that others also may fear. I charge thee before God, and the Lord Jesus Christ, and the elect angels, that thou observe these things without preferring one before another, doing nothing by partiality. Lay hands suddenly on no man, neither be partaker of other men's sins: keep thyself pure. Drink no longer water, but use a little wine for thy stomach's sake and thine often infirmities. Some men's sins are open beforehand, going before to judgment; and some men they follow after. Likewise also the good works of some are manifest beforehand; and they that are otherwise cannot be hid (1 Tim. 5:20-25).

Let us look at these verses just as we read them. "Them that sin rebuke before all, that others also may fear." Paul told Timothy that when something was wrong, he should talk about it. He should tell it openly. He should point out what God's Word says. That is the only way in which the preacher can help others avoid doing the same wrong. If wrong conduct is condoned in silence, then others may fall into that same snare. Someone may ask, "Are you saying it ought to be spoken out in the open?" That is where the sin was committed. That is where the remarks should be made.

"I charge thee before God, and the Lord Jesus Christ, and the elect angels, that thou observe these things without preferring one before another, doing nothing by partiality." You can hardly think of anything more solemn than that. This is calling on all the beings in heaven to witness this whole matter. It is calling a man to live his life in the presence of the invisible realities of God and of heaven. Paul is saying to Timothy, "I want you to take care of this, remembering that almighty God is seeing everything that you do. I want you to be very careful when you do these things that you do not let personal consideration enter into your thinking." The minister must be scrupulously fair. God is no respecter of persons, and the minister cannot be any respecter of persons. Since he is acting in the name of Christ, he must act fairly.

"Lay hands suddenly on no man." That gesture in the New Testament seems to be a matter of endorsing persons or giving a person a certain responsibility. Ruling Elders put their hands on the officers in the congregation who were ordained to a certain task. Today we put hands on the minister when we ordain him to the ministry, and we lay our hands on the elders and the deacons when we ordain them to their responsibility in their offices. Paul is saying to Timothy, "Lay hands suddenly on no man," which is to say, "Do not be hasty about endorsing anybody," and "Neither be partaker of other men's sins." Because others do it does not make it right. A thing is right or wrong in itself. Timothy is to be straightforward and honest about his part. "Keep thyself pure." He is to make it a point to be deliberate in his choices. He is to be careful in the stance that he takes before the public.

Then Paul goes on to say something about which I am sure many people have wondered. "Drink no longer water, but use a little wine for thy stomach's sake and thine often infirmities." Regardless of how one or another may push this matter in its interpretation, it is obvious that Paul is asking him to use this wine as medicine, as it was commonly used in that day. Such medicine would be proper just as much as any other medicine. Timothy was a good man about whom Paul said that he had no man like-minded (I have been inclined to point out he was probably one of the greatest believers in the New Testament). This good man was sickly. I am sure you have heard persons imply that if you were a real believer you would not have any illness, that if you had real faith you would not be sick. I think that any person who is tempted to accept that as true, should look very closely at this verse. Here was a man who had infirmities, and Paul told him to take some medicine for them, and that medicine was wine.

The closing portion of this passage in another translation

reads thus: "The sins of some men are conspicuous, openly evident to all eyes, going before them to the judgment (seat) and proclaiming their sentence in advance; but the sins of others appear later, following the offender to the bar of judgment and coming into view there. So also good deeds are evident and conspicuous, and even when they are not, they cannot remain hidden (indefinitely)." This has been translated into these words: "Remember that some men, even pastors, lead sinful lives and everyone knows it. In such situations you can do something about it. But in other cases only the Judgment Day will reveal the terrible truth. In the same way, everyone knows how much good some pastors do, but sometimes their good deeds aren't known until long afterward." The minister is to deal with sin by rebuking and with righteousness by esteeming, but he sees only some of the sin and some of the righteousness. There will be more sin than he knows, and there will be more righteousness than he knows. He is not the final judge. But when anything is openly seen, it should be openly treated. If it is sin it should be rebuked, and if it is righteousness, it should be appreciated and approved.

Chapter 26

THE GOSPEL ACCEPTS THE SOCIAL ORDER AS IT IS

Do you realize that the Gospel does not undertake to change any social pattern?

> Let as many servants as are under the yoke count their own masters worthy of all honour, that the name of God and his doctrine be not blasphemed. And they that have believing masters, let them not despise them, because they are brethren; but rather do them service, because they are faithful and beloved, partakers of the benefit. These things teach and exhort. If any man teach otherwise, and consent not to wholesome words, even the words of our Lord Jesus Christ, and to the doctrine which is according to godliness; he is proud, knowing nothing, but doting about questions and strifes of words, whereof cometh envy, strife, railings, evil surmisings, perverse disputings of men of corrupt minds, and destitute of the truth, supposing that gain is godliness: from such withdraw thyself (1 Tim. 6:1-5).

I personally think that the Gospel of the Lord Jesus Christ was involved in the modern world in the abolition of slavery. But the truth is that neither Jesus of Nazareth nor any of His followers in the New Testament ever spoke against it. This is not to say that these people favored slavery, but it is to say that slavery as such was not the problem. They were concerned about the soul's relationship with God. Some of the believers were slaves, and some of the believers were masters; and the Gospel was intended for both. It would not be any different as far as the Lord was concerned. Master and slave would be reconciled to God through the Lord Jesus Christ, and each one in the Lord Jesus Christ would stand equal before God.

"Let as many servants as are under the yoke count their own masters worthy of all honor." Being under the yoke meant that they were like slaves, and they were to count their own masters worthy of all honor. This was not limited to the good masters. If

The Gospel Accepts the Social Order As It Is   95

a servant was inwardly moved by the Holy Spirit of God, he would serve his master with respect and consideration. In so doing the believers would be paying tribute to God, not to the master. Apparently there was to be no tendency in the servant toward rebellion. The slave was not to feel resentful because he was a slave. The believer was to accept the local, practical situation in which he was the servant as ordered by God, and he would act as a servant should act to the honor and glory of God.

Often, when a social problem comes up, we hear in a discussion of the local situation, "God certainly wouldn't want matters to be like that!" Wait a minute! What are you saying? If God did not want matters to be like that, He could change them. If all those people dropped dead, it would be all over. But they are living. Why? Because God let them live. Consider this: God could do differently. I do not think I will ever fully understand while I am here in this life why God made this world as it is; but I believe He made these human beings as they are and put them here as they are, and He watches over them. He knows all about them, and God is in control. To be submissive in the situation is actually a testimony of my faith in God.

It is easy to say we trust God when we are fortunate. It is easy to say this if by comparison with others we are well off, but that is not actually doing justice to what I have just said. What I wanted to say to you is that any believer in Christ in his particular local situation, whatever that situation may be, will be able to accept that situation as something that God allowed to be. To put it on a purely academic basis and from the standpoint of overall judgment, one could very well say God would not want sin. But God has seen fit to allow it, and He is able to overrule and to bring His will to pass. To be submissive in the situation in which I am is actually a testimony of my faith in God. Any master is worthy of all honor, not because of the man, but because of the position of being master.

Then Paul goes on to say, "And they that have believing masters (because some masters actually believed in Christ), let them not despise them." The believers who themselves were servants were not to despise the owners who might also be believers. This refers to a common, natural tendency that you can feel wherever you look: The boss is something bad. Now a believing person will gladly render all due respect to a believing master. It is not his business to decide whether that master is good or bad in the sight of God. It is my business to conduct myself with respect and honor toward the person I am serving. If I need to make any assumptions I will assume that the person is a good person, and I will act that way. He may not be, but that is God's business, not mine.

"If any man teach otherwise, and consent not to wholesome words." What kind of words would be wholesome words? Words that promote health are wholesome. "Even the words of our Lord Jesus Christ, and to the doctrine which is according to godliness." The doctrine of our Lord Jesus Christ is according to godliness and refers to the way in which you are living. In the last analysis, as far as any teaching or preaching is concerned, the hallmark of truth is godly living, godly doing, and godly being. That is the evidence that it is real.

The man who consents not to wholesome words, "he is proud, knowing nothing, but doting about questions and strifes of words, whereof cometh envy, strife, railings, evil surmisings, perverse disputings of men of corrupt minds, and destitute of the truth, supposing that gain is godliness: from such withdraw thyself." The minister must be careful whom he accepts as his companion. There will be men who are not willing to submit to the demands of godliness and righteousness but who want to be accepted as interpreters of the truth. Paul might say, "If there is any person who does not consent to these rules for his personal relationship with God, who is not in favor of humbly submitting himself to other people, that person is proud, knowing nothing" (I think we could say "nothing of the will of God"). This person would seem to imply that anything on which to make a profit is the thing that is good. Paul says to Timothy, "From such withdraw thyself." He was not to have anything to do with such people.

Chapter 27

STRIVING TO BE RICH IS DANGEROUS

Can you understand how the inner drive to excel over others in this world is actually dangerous to spiritual life?

> But godliness with contentment is great gain. For we brought nothing into this world, and it is certain we can carry nothing out. And having food and raiment let us be therewith content. But they that will be rich fall into temptation and snare, and into many foolish and hurtful lusts, which drown men in destruction and perdition (1 Tim. 6:6-9).

It is not easy, even for a believer, to recognize the danger in doing something that everybody approves. If everybody is for it, would it be all right? Maybe not. It is possible that something that would have widespread approval among men might be an abomination in the sight of the Lord. On every side esteem is given to the winner. It is an old principle in school management to stir up competition among the students, and rivalry among those who are in the classes. The teachers do this to get motivation. They want these young people to study. They want them to work. So they set out the goal that if the students will do thus and so, they will be ahead of others. Thus we lay all our emphasis on winning.

I was a school teacher for many years. I taught public school for about nine years off and on. After that I became a college professor for three years; and then I was for twenty-seven years a professor in seminary. I have been teaching much of my life, and I know it has been a constant problem to motivate the students to study. But as time has gone on, and even back in the days when I was in the classroom of the public school, I came to understand that this matter of emphasizing the winner, of giving first place and high regard to the person who had the highest score, has something about it that is very unhealthy.

As I came to the end of my career in teaching school, I had this in mind more and more. I set up schemes wherein the individual competed with himself. I made it a point to pay special attention to how much better he was doing this week than he did last week, and how much better he was doing this month than he did last month. I graded the students on the percentage of improvement that they made. Within reason as well as I could, I would not give the award to the number one winner. I gave the award to anybody who achieved a certain level of performance. There were times when I would have twelve students to whom I gave out as many as ten awards. Yes, they had done more than was required, and each got his award.

Though I had this feeling in my very bones, I did not realize the spiritual significance of this. The old principle in school management leads us to have contests. The worst thing about a contest is not that somebody is going to win. The worst thing is that somebody is going to lose. As for exhibitions, they discourage activity. The boy or girl who is successful does not need the exhibition. The boy or girl who is not successful is discouraged and feels downhearted. Fame and fortune, which are commonly used as beacons to guide and to arouse and to motivate, are actually misleading. Let me emphasize what Paul says, "Godliness with contentment is great gain." What does that mean? You are well-off if your life is right in the sight of God and you are contented.

Then Paul goes ahead and gives his argument: "We brought nothing into this world, and it is certain we can carry nothing out." If a person were going to pile up money, why? He will have to leave it. If he works to win some big award, why? He will have to leave it. Someone else will get it after him. Paul pointed to this truth: "We brought nothing into this world, and it is certain we can carry nothing out. And having food and raiment let us be therewith content." Someone may say, "If you followed that as a way of doing things, you certainly would not have much done." I am not so sure about that. And anyway, that is not the main interest. I would like to have a heart at peace and a mind at rest. Having food and raiment, I could be content. This is profound, simple, and amazing.

Striving to Be Rich Is Dangerous

Paul is not the only one who said that.

> Yea, I hated all my labour which I had taken under the sun: because I should leave it unto the man that shall be after me. And who knoweth whether he shall be a wise man or a fool? yet shall he have rule over all my labour wherein I have laboured, and wherein I have shewed myself wise under the sun. This is also vanity. Therefore I went about to cause my heart to despair of all the labour which I took under the sun. For there is a man whose labour is in wisdom, and in knowledge, and in equity; yet to a man that hath not laboured therein shall he leave it for his portion. This also is vanity and a great evil. For what hath man of all his labour, and of the vexation of his heart, wherein he hath laboured under the sun? For all his days are sorrows, and his travail grief; yea, his heart taketh not rest in the night. This is also vanity. There is nothing better for a man, than that he should eat and drink, and that he should make his soul enjoy good in his labour. This also I saw, that it was from the hand of God. For who can eat, or who else can hasten hereunto, more than I? For God giveth to a man that is good in his sight wisdom, and knowledge, and joy: but to the sinner he giveth travail, to gather and to heap up, that he may give to him that is good before God. This also is vanity and vexation of spirit (Eccl. 2:18-26).

Then look also at these words: "There is a sore evil which I have seen under the sun, namely, riches kept for the owners thereof to their hurt" (Eccl. 5:13).

Here is the Gospel answer to this issue: "But they that will be rich fall into temptation and a snare, and into many foolish and hurtful lusts, which drown men in destruction and perdition." They that will be rich in business are tempted to dishonesty. They that want to be rich in prestige are tempted to flattery, to showing favoritism. Those that want to be rich in friends are tempted to steal to keep up their standards. With such people, everything goes. Paul warns all these people. He admonishes believers not to try to become first, high up, and rich in this world. They can get into trouble that way.

Chapter 28

PAUL'S ADVICE TO TIMOTHY

Can you see that, even when a believer is dedicated to do the will of God as led by the Holy Spirit, he may yet benefit by good advice from other believers?

There was never any doubt in Paul's mind about Timothy being a committed man. Timothy was entirely devoted to the Lord, and in his own spirit he sought to do the will of God. If a person had an inward relationship with God by trusting in the Lord Jesus Christ, so that he knew according to the Scriptures that the Holy Spirit of God was within him, would he need any advice from other believers? Should anybody talk to him about what he is going to do? Actions need to be learned. Now we shall see how Paul was advising Timothy.

> For the love of money is the root of all evil: which while some coveted after, they have erred from the faith, and pierced themselves through with many sorrows. But thou, O man of God, flee these things; and follow after righteousness, godliness, faith, love, patience, meekness. Fight the good fight of faith, lay hold on eternal life, whereunto thou art also called, and hast professed a good profession before many witnesses. I give thee charge in the sight of God, who quickeneth all things, and before Christ Jesus, who before Pontius Pilate witnessed a good confession; that thou keep this commandment without spot, unrebukable, until the appearing of our Lord Jesus Christ: which in his times he shall shew, who is the blessed and only Potentate, the King of kings, and Lord of lords; who only hath immortality, dwelling in the light which no man can approach unto; whom no man hath seen, nor can see: to whom be honour and power everlasting (1 Tim. 6:10-16).

Let us look at the items that Paul mentioned. "For the love of money is the root of all evil: which while some coveted after, they have erred from the faith, and pierced themselves

Paul's Advice to Timothy 101

through with many sorrows." This does not say that money is evil. It says the love of money is the root of all evil. Another fact we should notice is this: the love of money is not the peculiar affliction of the rich. It is a common disease among all people. A great many people love money who do not have it. Money is a symbol, and the love of money is the desire to have what you need to do as you please.

How can the love of money be the root of all evil? Anything that exalts self is evil. You will remember how the Lord Jesus put it: "If any man will come after me, let him deny himself." So when I am discussing evil and interpreting evil, my argument is simple. Our Lord taught that if any will come after Him, let him deny himself. The opposite of that would be to serve himself, and that is evil. Now money will serve self. With money I can do things, and if I love money, that indicates that I have no inclination to deny myself.

Even in Paul's time, even in the early church, there were some among the believers who had erred from the faith. Earlier in this letter to Timothy, Paul talked about heretics, but not here. The believer is deviating from the Gospel and turning away from the message of God when he has his interest in money, or in that which would enable him to do as he pleases. No details are given, if you will notice, and Paul does not spell out how they erred from the faith. This is in keeping with Paul's practice of giving no details of evil things.

But let us notice how he deals with virtues. The moment that he has said, "Flee from these things," he goes on to say, "Follow after righteousness, godliness, faith, love, patience, meekness. Fight the good fight of faith, lay hold on eternal life, whereunto thou art also called." When I fight the good fight of faith, what is the good fight of faith about? It is about me. I am to deny me. I am to yield myself into the will of God by way of the cross of Calvary. I am to yield myself to be crucified with Christ. How can I possibly do that? By laying hold on eternal life which is the life of God. Let me take advantage of the fact that God has given me the Holy Spirit within me, and let me be led by that. This was in the Lord's will for me when He called me. He offered to come and help me. That is what God wanted me to have.

"And hast professed a good profession before many

witnesses." This is like saying, "I solemnly call upon you to live up to the expectations that you shared when you started." This is a way of saying to this young man, "When you started out to serve God, what did you have in mind? You had in mind that you would yield yourself to the will of God and let God work in you. Now you need to bring your whole experience into the presence of God who gives life to everything, and into the presence of Christ Jesus who humbly yielded Himself to die and be buried. You should set yourself to this task. You should accept this responsibility. You are a minister; you are a believer, a witness. You should show forth the things of the Lord. Then you should do all these extraordinary works of self-denial and wisdom, by the indwelling Christ who will enable you. You should keep this up until Christ Jesus appears in person. He is coming, and you can be sure He will make it worthwhile. His personal greatness can be the basis of your assurance." This is the way Paul talked to Timothy. If you and I believe in the Lord Jesus Christ, let us follow Paul's advice, yielding ourselves to the will of God, trusting in Him.

Chapter 29

HOW SHOULD THE RICH BE CAUTIOUS?

Can a rich person do anything to win the blessing of God?

> Charge them that are rich in this world, that they be not highminded, nor trust in uncertain riches, but in the living God, who giveth us richly all things to enjoy; that they do good, that they be rich in good works, ready to distribute, willing to communicate; laying up in store for themselves a good foundation against the time to come, that they may lay hold on eternal life (1 Tim. 6:17-19).

Being rich means having more of what enables you to do things than others have around you. It may be money, but it need not be only money. A girl can be rich in her beauty. A man can be rich in his strength. A student can be rich in his brains. Anybody can be rich in friends, or perhaps in family. No doubt many people are rich who do not realize it. It is such an easy thing when you are healthy and well to forget health. The person who is sick appreciates health and longs for it. It would be an easy thing if a person had all the money that he needed, so he could forget all about money. But the poor man does not forget about money. He is very much conscious of the fact that he does not have money.

Not everybody has as much as everybody else. Some folks are rich. Jesus of Nazareth warned about this. He pointed out, "Verily I say unto you that a rich man shall hardly enter into the kingdom of heaven." I know that not everybody is rich, but I am satisfied that many of us are far richer than we realize. We may not realize the problems that come to us because we are rich, in that we have an advantage over other people. Folks with advantage often forget that they have the advantage and are open to snares and troubles. The words of Jesus of Nazareth, ". . . a rich man shall hardly enter into the kingdom of heaven," mean that while a rich man may enter into the kingdom of heaven, the word "hardly" means only with effort.

You will remember the occasion of that remark. The rich young man had come to Jesus of Nazareth and asked Him, "Good Master, what shall I do that I might inherit eternal life?" Jesus of Nazareth said to him finally, "If you really want to come with Me, go, sell what thou hast and give to the poor, take up thy cross and follow Me." Examine those words to learn what He was telling the young man. "Use your wealth on behalf of the needy. Then you can come and follow me."

An interpretation of this particular passage of Scripture was given to me many years ago by Dr. R. A. Torrey. You may have read his books. He was a great evangelist and a great Bible teacher. Dr. Torrey, talking to us students at the Bible Institute, pointed out one day that many of us were rich in ways we did not even appreciate. Then he went on to say that these riches would tempt us to be proud. Was it not true that many a young man who is a star athlete becomes proud and arrogant? Was it not true that the pretty girl can become vain? The person who is in the midst of many friends can become conceited. The smart student, up near the top or at the very top of the class, would he not be inclined to become overbearing and proud? Dr. Torrey pointed out that if we do have money we should not throw it away. If one were good-looking, he should not disfigure himself. If one were physically strong, he should not cripple himself.

But how could we possibly overcome the danger that was involved? We could use our advantage to help the poor. That pretty girl could make it a point to cultivate the fellowship of girls in her class who were not attractive. She could take time to be with them. Any of us who were healthy could take time to visit the sick and be with them. If any of us had enough money so that we could buy anything we wanted, we could take some of that money and give it to the poor. We could share with them. Dr. Torrey pointed out that if a person used his money to help the poor, his money would be a means of blessing. If a believer will use her attractiveness to spend some time with the neglected ones, her attractiveness can be a means of blessing. Anyone who is smart and at the top of his class could take time out to help the slow student and fellowship with him.

Then his cleverness would be a source of blessing. In that way, Dr. Torrey told us, we could keep our riches from doing us harm. We could actually sanctify them, because we set them apart for the service of God. Our wealth could be a source of blessing.

Now let us consider what the Apostle Paul went on to say to Timothy: "Charge them that are rich in this world, that they be not high-minded (not conceited, nor arrogant), nor trust in uncertain riches (that is, do not put your confidence in money even if you could use it), but in the living God, who giveth us richly all things to enjoy." Then Paul goes on to say, "That they do good." That is what I have been talking about. The believer should use his advantages to help people who do not have the advantage. ". . . that they be rich in good works, ready to distribute, willing to communicate" (gracious, willing to talk with other people).

"Laying up in store for themselves a good foundation against the time to come." What is meant by "the time to come"? One thing in the time to come is the Judgment Day. Everyone will come before the judgment seat of the Lord Jesus Christ to be judged for things that were done in the body. When that time comes, when believers meet the Lord, those things that the believer has done on behalf of others not as fortunate as he will be precious to him then. "That they may lay hold on eternal life," making use of the grace of God, yielding themselves into His will. Paul would tell Timothy, this young minister and young believer, that he should never let fortunate circumstances lull him into careless confidence in himself.

Chapter 30

THE DANGER IN SCIENCE

Do you realize the danger in seeking an explanation for everything? It is rather sobering to think that, if a believer does not follow the Gospel of the Lord Jesus Christ and walk after Him in the ways of God, the believer is in danger of being misled. The way in which God allows things to develop is such that a believer is never safe apart from personal fellowship with the living Lord Jesus Christ.

When Paul was writing to Timothy he warned that some had already turned aside. Some that profess to follow science have erred concerning the truth. Paul warns Timothy to watch out because in this world nobody is safe except in the Lord Jesus Christ. He is the Strong Tower, and if the believer enters into Him he is safe. But outside of Him no believer is safe. The believer will be beset by "the enemy (who) goeth about as a roaring lion seeking whom he may devour."

> O Timothy, keep that which is committed to thy trust, avoiding profane and vain babblings, and oppositions of science falsely so called: which some professing have erred concerning the faith. Grace be with thee. Amen (1 Tim. 6:20-21).

We should understand that the word "science" as used here is a general term which refers to a frame of mind. When Paul speaks of the "oppositions of science falsely so called" he is not talking of physics or chemistry or biology or geology or physiology. He is not talking about these modern advanced systematic disciplines of scientific thinking. He is talking about a certain mood, a certain frame of mind, that he refers to as science. It is that mood, that attitude of mind in which the individual is searching for a cause, that is the very basis of all science. We do well to remember that the infinite, eternal things of God are beyond the measure of man's mind. No kind or nature of scientific research is ever going to arrive at the truth of the things of God, because the things of God originate in His will. The ways of God are past finding out. Even when He works by His Holy Spirit the things of the Spirit are not known to us. They are hidden, so far as we are concerned. Any human being seeking to understand the ways of God so he can give a comprehensive explanation is wrong. He is trying to do the impossible. We could say stop right there. For the human being to attempt this shows not only an individual arrogance on his part, but it shows a total misconception of God. That man does not appreciate God. It is like trying to control the sunlight with a fishnet. It cannot be done.

Paul wrote, "O Timothy, keep that which is committed to thy trust, avoiding profane and vain babblings, and oppositions of science falsely so called." When Paul brought in Timothy's name, this made it personal. This is how God would put in your name. God will tell you as a believer to keep that which is committed to your trust. When the word "keep" is used here, it means guard, preserve, cherish it; hold it carefully in both hands; take good care; watch over it. Do not let anything deteriorate while it is in your hands. Keep that which is committed to your trust. What is committed to the trust of the believer? The Gospel, the work of the Spirit, are committed to each believer, and he is to guard them.

"Avoid profane and vain babblings." One can ask oneself, is that the result of science falsely so-called? When you use the word "profane" here, you do not mean blasphemy nor using profanity in the sense of using the name of God carelessly. Profane is a word that indicates you are taking holy things and making them common, or taking infinite things and making them finite. It is taking eternal things and making them temporal. It is treating heavenly things as if they belonged on this earth. That is the meaning of "profane," taking some great eternal, infinite, spiritual reality and handling it as if it were something in this world.

I can remember many years ago when I entered the university. I had decided that I would study in the field of the social sciences, and I had selected psychology as my major. In my first classes in psychology I could feel that the professor was indicating that science was very, very dependable; but faith was something else, and you could not go by faith because it was just imaginary. After I listened to him for some time, I went up to him to clarify things, as well as to give expression to my own feelings. I told him that I was not able to follow his presentation. He wanted to know why. I said, "You talk as if a person could not be scientific about faith. You talk as if one could not be scientific about spiritual things. You talk as though in order to be scientific something would have to be physical. Couldn't something be scientific that was spiritual?"

In that same class on another occasion the professor indicated in a rather disparaging way that nobody today would accept a doctrine such as predestination. Then he went right on in the lecture and presented determinism from a scientific point of view, saying that where you are determines what you are, because you are that way. When he had finished I again went up to him privately. I said, "I don't understand why you react so violently against predestination because you think it binds a person, when you turn right around and accept determinism which binds you for sure." There was no real answer to my remark. Paul says some have been so influenced by apparent scientific "opposition of science falsely so called" that they have fallen into error.

So we see that throughout this letter, the letter of First Timothy, Paul has sought to guide Timothy in his responsibility of leading the believers, the congregation, into fruitful, worthy witnessing in their living for God. All the way through in this last study he has been warning Timothy to remember that the ways of God are beyond finding out.

Second Timothy

Chapter 1

PAUL'S GREETING TO TIMOTHY

Can you see how faith in the Lord Jesus Christ in the heart of a friend or a loved one is reason for joy and gratitude to God?
Paul had many fellow workers serving with him in telling the Gospel, but none that he appreciated more than Timothy.

> For I have no man likeminded, who will naturally care for your state. For all seek their own, not the things which are Jesus Christ's. But ye know the proof of him, that, as a son with the father, he hath served with me in the gospel (Phil. 2:20-22).

This is a way of saying in our language, "He is the most wonderful believer I know." That is what Paul said about Timothy. Now we are going to study the second epistle of Paul to Timothy, perhaps the last epistle that Paul wrote.

> Paul, an apostle of Jesus Christ by the will of God, according to the promise of life which is in Christ Jesus, to Timothy, my dearly beloved son: Grace, mercy, and peace, from God the Father and Christ Jesus our Lord. I thank God, whom I serve from my forefathers with pure conscience, that without ceasing I have remembrance of thee in my prayers night and day; greatly desiring to see thee, being mindful of thy tears, that I may be filled with joy (2 Tim. 1:1-4).

I hope you see the earnest warmth of Paul's heart toward Timothy. When Paul reveals here the basis of his great joy in this young preacher, he speaks of himself, saying "an apostle of Jesus Christ by the will of God, according to the promise of life which is in Christ Jesus." Now the fact that he knew that he was an apostle means that he realized he was sent from the Lord Jesus Christ. "By the will of God," means, I think, that Paul would always have in mind, "Being an apostle was not my idea. I can take no credit for being in this work, for having this mission. This was given to me. I didn't deserve it and I didn't particularly ask for it, because at the time it was given to me I didn't even want it."

"By the will of God, according to the promise of life which is in Christ Jesus." When I was preparing this study I saw something here I had never really seen before: "the promise of life which is in Christ Jesus." I am sure many people have the feeling that if they believe in the Lord Jesus Christ they are going to be blessed, and I am sure some earnest people willingly expand their understanding of that blessing to include everything. Therefore people talk about the Lord Jesus blessing them when they were on a journey, when they were in their car, or perhaps when they were in their business. Now I do not doubt that there is a certain element of truth possible in all of that. You could have said that God watched over me in His providence, and led me, because I want to bring something to your mind. But what Christ Jesus particularly offers to me is eternal life. I am to have the life of God in my soul.

When I have the life of God in my soul, I will live in this world just like anybody else, under the same laws and circumstances. You may have known me to say that it is just as hot for a believer as it is for an unbeliever, and if I neglect and foolishly leave my clothing out in the rain, it will get wet. It is just as cold for a believer as it is for an unbeliever. Circumstances do not change because of your personal faith. The road will be just as rough and bumpy if you are a believer, as it was rough and bumpy when you were an unbeliever. You may ask me, "Well, isn't there some difference in the experiences the believer has?" There may well be. God may in His providence grant that His believers will have a little better road or a little smoother way, but we will be wrong if we think that the promises of God in the Lord Jesus Christ will spare the believer from trouble or from difficulties.

I expect that if I foolishly step into a hole, I will sink; and if I bump into a chair I will get hurt. In other words, just because I am a believer does not change the processes of nature in any way. What it does mean is that I will have the inward grace that comes from God to face all the issues of living. I will live in just the same situation other people live in, but I will have something going for me. I will have almighty God working for me.

Paul's Greeting to Timothy

The one blessing promised is eternal life which is in Christ Jesus. This eternal life is not given as an addition to me. If my name should happen to be Tom Brown, and I become a believer in the Lord Jesus Christ, I do not add to me anything. That is not the idea. I get something that replaces me, that substitutes for me. I understand myself, and I am not Tom Brown anymore. People call me Tom Brown, but I am now a child of God. This is what I can have in mind when I think of the life that is in Christ Jesus. It is not in addition to me and my life, but is a substitution for me and my life. Now I have said far more on this than I can explain in this book. You think about it, and just remember that the Lord Jesus Christ is not something added. He is Someone who takes over and controls.

"Grace, mercy, and peace, from God the Father and Christ Jesus our Lord." Grace is the inward enablement to do His will. We may see the will of God before us, and it does not change for a believer or an unbeliever. Whatever the will of God is, that is what is to be done. If you want to know the will of God, from a human point of view, a very simple way would be to read the Ten Commandments. There it is. There is much more than that, but still that is a good way to get started.

How is a person going to do the will of God? The only way a person can begin to walk in the ways of God is to deny himself. The only way he can walk in the ways of God is to reckon himself dead, and nobody naturally wants to do that. So he turns to the Lord Jesus Christ, he believes in Him, and God gives him His grace, an inward strength, enablement, to do God's will the way He wants it done. "Mercy" is that which comes through God's providence. God would be good to the believer. God would be kind to him. God is touched with the feelings of that person's infirmities. God will help him. God is merciful; we must not ever forget that. "And peace"—a believer in Christ can have peace with God and he can have peace in himself, because he reckons himself to be dead, and he has committed himself to God. He can have peace in his circumstances, since he takes all things as coming from God. He can have peace about the future, he trusts in God, because God knows the end from the beginning. The believer can have peace with God through the Lord Jesus Christ. So we have grace, mercy, and peace from God the Father. By the way, He is the Father of Jesus Christ, and He is the Father of me when I am a believer. He is our Master. He directs our steps.

"I thank God, whom I serve from my forefathers with pure conscience." This is worth looking at. Here late in life Paul reminds Timothy, "I have always walked honestly before God. There was a time in my life when I was an unbeliever. I did everything I possibly could against the name of Jesus Christ. But I was ignorant. However, I was honest and I was sincere, and I am sincere now." Paul never did criticize the life that he had when he was at home with his family. He had grown up as a young man very earnest and very zealous, wanting to do the will of God, "Whom I serve from my forefathers." He did not know about Jesus Christ; but he had a pure conscience, meaning to say he had nothing to hide. He says, "I thank God . . . without ceasing I have remembrance of thee in my prayers night and day." Paul prayed anytime he thought of Timothy, always, night and day. This does not mean that he was praying continuously; but that whenever he prayed, Timothy was in his heart and mind.

"Greatly desiring to see thee, being mindful of thy tears, that I may be filled with joy." What would the tears of Timothy indicate? Would they not indicate Timothy's earnest, sincere, tender heart? Could this not mean that Timothy was concerned about the lost, and that he was concerned about the suffering? He cared, and Paul delighted to see this in him. It strengthened and encouraged Paul to see this young preacher so earnestly and so sincerely seeking the goodness of God and the grace of God for the people. This was the effect of Timothy. Paul would get personal blessing and strength by fellowship with this earnest believer.

Chapter 2

PAUL'S ADMONITION TO TIMOTHY

Can you understand why an older believer would urge a younger believer to endure affliction willingly because of his faith in the Lord?

> When I call to remembrance the unfeigned faith that is in thee, which dwelt first in thy grandmother Lois, and thy mother Eunice; and I am persuaded that in thee also. Wherefore I put thee in remembrance that thou stir up the gift of God, which is in thee by the putting on of my hands. For God hath not given us the spirit of fear; but of power, and of love, and of a sound mind. Be not thou therefore ashamed of the testimony of our Lord, nor of me his prisoner: but be thou partaker of the afflictions of the gospel according to the power of God (2 Tim. 1:5-8).

Paul was blessed in the fellowship that he had with Timothy, his younger partner, and in the service that Timothy rendered. Fellowship with Timothy brought to Paul fullness of joy because of Timothy's faith. This is an interesting thought. I would have thought that Paul rejoiced because of Timothy's work; but he rejoiced because of Timothy's faith, which he described as genuine and sincere. "When I call to remembrance the unfeigned faith that is in thee," that word "unfeigned" means unpretended, sincere, genuine, real, not "put on." Timothy had real faith. Paul went on to say, "which dwelt first in thy grandmother Lois, and thy mother Eunice; and I am persuaded that in thee also." We could raise a question at this point: do you think the faith of parents affects the faith of their children? Apparently this is really, soberly, honestly, terribly true.

The faith of parents affects the faith of their children. The reason that is so awesome is because it is likewise true that unbelief of parents affects the children. In the course of my lifetime I have witnessed some sad examples of this very thing. When I was pastor I found time and again that when a man did not want to join the church, he had a father who did not belong to the church. Invariably when you come across a man in his thirties or his forties, who is still not a member of the church, and you ask him to join the church, he will hesitate. If you dig down, scrape the surface a little, you will find out that his father did not belong to the church. That happens over and over again. It is regrettable but it is true. I could wish it were different, but there is something real about it. That is the underside of the coin in the matter of parental influence.

But there is a topside of this coin that we are looking at: the wonderful truth is that when the parents are believers, there is a strong tendency upon the part of the children to turn themselves to God. Paul's comment here includes the intimation that strong faith in the parents insures stronger faith in the children and in grandchildren.

Faith in the heart of another, by the way, cannot ever be seen directly. Paul could not see this faith in Timothy. There is not some particular sign that shows if a man is a believer; but you could watch him, you could hear his words, you could see his conduct, and you would know. Paul was persuaded that Timothy was a genuine believer. He was all the more persuaded in this because he knew the faith that was in the grandmother and in the mother. Is not that an amazing thing!

Apparently Timothy's family had heard the Gospel. I am inclined to think that the grandmother first believed, then the mother believed, and so Timothy also believed. By the way, Timothy is one person serving in the New Testament and written about in the book of Acts of whom there is no record of his conversion. No time is mentioned when Timothy was an unbeliever and then was changed over to faith. Apparently this is a young lad who was brought up "in the nurture and admonition of the Lord."

Because Paul was so sure of Timothy's grounded faith, he urges Timothy to be active in his service. "Wherefore I put thee in remembrance that thou stir up the gift of God, which is in thee by the putting on of my hands. For God hath not given us the spirit of fear; but of power, and of love, and of a sound mind. Be not thou therefore ashamed of the testimony of our

Lord, nor of me his prisoner: but be thou partaker of the afflictions of the gospel according to the power of God." That is the whole passage which presents one thought. When Paul wrote, "I put thee in remembrance that thou stir up the gift of God, which is in thee," he raises a question. What is this gift of God which was given to Timothy by the laying on of the hands of the apostles? It is doubtful that this gift of God refers to any inward spiritual power or grace that Timothy had in himself. I am not inclined to think that any minister of the Gospel can transfer or communicate into another man's heart any special grace. There are some who think this happens. There are denominations who count on this in their ritual or procedure. They seem to think that by the laying on of hands a special benefit, a gift of grace, is given to special persons. Some have a special word for that. It is called a "sacerdotal" practice, when people actually try to give sacredness or consecration to others.

But if Paul did not mean that, then what was it? It may have been like a commission. In my own denomination we lay hands on people when they are committed to a certain task. It may be that Paul in laying his hands on Timothy committed Timothy to a certain task. Timothy had been given a certain task to perform, and the stirring up of this gift would be recalling it to mind. Paul urged him, "For God hath not given us the spirit of fear; but of power, and of love, and of a sound mind." Apparently the task that he had given Timothy would involve the need for power, love, and a sound mind. Thus Timothy would be effective in what he had to do. He would be gracious in his procedure, and he would be reasonable (or shall I say intelligent) in the way in which he went about things. Because all this was true, he would get up and get at it. This seems to be what Paul wrote to this young man. "Be not thou therefore ashamed of the testimony of our Lord, nor of me his prisoner: but be thou partaker of the afflictions of the gospel according to the power of God." Apparently that was part of what was to be his task. Timothy's commission was to preach the testimony of Jesus Christ, and the testimony of Paul the prisoner of Jesus Christ. This was what Timothy had been left to do.

What would be the testimony of Jesus Christ? It would be that no man on his own can get right with God. A man must be born again. Only by the help of God and by the grace of God can any human being ever walk acceptably to God. That is the testimony of Jesus Christ. What would be the testimony of Paul? Salvation is only through Christ by faith. It could perhaps be expressed in some other way; but apparently Paul is saying to Timothy, "In your ministry which you now have in hand, I gave you and I assigned you to this task: you are to tell the people about the Lord Jesus Christ and tell them about my testimony, where I stand, that salvation is only possible through Jesus Christ."

"But be thou partaker of the afflictions of the gospel according to the power of God." The message that Timothy was to give would stir up opposition. If he would declare this Gospel, if he would tell the people of the world the things that the Lord Jesus came to do, and the things that the Apostle Paul preached, he would be persecuted. He would have suffering. So Paul calls on him, "Be thou partaker of the afflictions of the gospel according to the power of God." The Gospel according to the power of God is that a human being must be born again into resurrection life, that he may have the newness of life in Christ Jesus. This is what Paul preached. This is what Timothy was to preach. So Paul called on him to "stir up in himself the consciousness of this task that was given to him."

Chapter 3

PAUL'S SUSTAINING CONFIDENCE

Can confidence in the time of suffering be based upon personal conviction that God is able to accomplish His gracious purpose?

> Who hath saved us, and called us with a holy calling, not according to our works, but according to his own purpose and grace, which was given us in Christ Jesus before the world began, but is now made manifest by the appearing of our Saviour Jesus Christ, who hath abolished death, and hath brought life and immortality to light through the gospel: whereunto I am appointed a preacher, and an apostle, and a teacher of the Gentiles. For the which cause I also suffer these things: nevertheless I am not ashamed: for I know whom I have believed, and am persuaded that he is able to keep that which I have committed unto him against that day (2 Tim. 1:9-12).

We look to the Bible to learn about the ways of God with men. That God is holy and demands righteousness on the part of anyone looking for blessing is a natural thing for us to believe. This may be because parents demand a certain obedience from their children; anyone in charge of anything looks for certain proper conduct on the part of others involved in the project. All that is natural to man; so that since God is almighty over all and is sovereign, it seems right that He should demand that people would do His will, and that He would be the One who would be the Judge. Even the idea that "the soul that sinneth, it shall die" is easy enough to understand. Though it is a hard thing to face, and it is something that causes many, many people to live in dread, still there seems to be no question that it is right.

Some persons are in such a frame of mind that they blame God for their troubles. They think that it is wrong for God to punish the evil, but I do not think there are many such. The vast majority of people, certainly honest and sincere people, are inclined to think that it would be only right that the soul that sins should die. God is a God of grace and will do what is needed for man because of His grace and undeserved kindness toward man. While this seems wonderful, it actually offends man's pride.

Man would like to think he could help himself. And if he could help himself he could compare himself with others. Thus some would think they were better than others. This would be natural. But to have to confess that one is a sinner and is guilty in the sight of God offends man's pride. To understand all this, keep in mind that God planned before the world began that man would be saved not by his own efforts but by the grace of God. This needs to be laid down as a basic truth. Men show their resentment to God's plan by afflicting the witnesses, by persecuting the preachers, by being against anybody who says so. This is the way they did with Paul.

Paul went on to write that God has "saved us, and called us with a holy calling, not according to our works, but according to his own purpose and grace, which was given us in Christ Jesus before the world began." God always planned to save man through Christ. It never was in the plan of God that man would be strong enough or good enough or able in himself to qualify for the blessing of God and for eternal fellowship with God. God made man of the dust of the ground, so that he had his limitations right in himself. God planned that man should come to face his own inadequacy so that he might be moved to put his whole trust in God. Now this plan of God was manifest, that means it was shown, in the Savior Jesus Christ.

When Jesus Christ passed through death into eternal life, this showed God's plan for man. So far as this world is concerned, so far as the natural being is concerned, man must yield himself to die here, that he might live forever there. In order that man could understand this, God sent His own Son incarnate, made of a woman and made flesh, that He might suffer death for man and then by His resurrection show how man could be raised from the dead. Paul knew this, and he had seen this. Paul also knew that he was appointed a preacher, an apostle, and a teacher of the Gentiles. Notice these three functions. When he was appointed a preacher, Paul exhorted the people, urged the people, to take advantage of Christ's resurrection that they might not miss this opportunity to be saved. As an apostle, Paul was authoritative. What he said was true. He could tell it the way it was. He could define the plan of salvation clearly. As a teacher of the Gentiles he was a man who could patiently, willingly, gladly, humbly teach the Gentiles, who had never heard about these things at all. He would tell them that God would raise from the dead those who would put their trust in Him. This is the whole idea. It is not deciding for a man how he is going to act. Any man has a mind of his own, and he can act on his own; but to get him right with God is the big problem. This was Paul's mission, and now it was to be Timothy's task.

Though this ministry was by God's grace, somebody would object to it. There are two reasons for objecting to the Gospel. One is that the Gospel sees the individual as a sinner. This takes away any pride or glory man can have in himself. The second reason people are opposed to it is that they have ideas of their own. They have been teaching and preaching ideas of their own, and the Gospel cuts across that. It says they are wrong.

Paul wrote, "For the which cause I also suffer these things," such as being put in prison, being brought before Caesar, the kind of things that were happening to Paul when he wrote this letter. Because of his ministry Paul had been put in prison and indicted before the Roman court as a troublemaker. This is what happened to him. He said, "Nevertheless I am not ashamed." This is not referring to any emotion on Paul's part. That phrase "I am not ashamed" means "I am not put to shame" or in other words, "I am not embarrassed by this. I am not even frustrated by this." Paul was in the community to tell people about Jesus Christ; that was different from what they believed. If conflict and controversy arose, that was par for the course. That was the way it turned out. When it happened, Paul was thrown into prison. But he was not ashamed, he was not upset by that. He was not embarrassed.

He went on to make a remarkable statement that has become famous. "For I know whom I have believed, and am persuaded that he is able to keep that which I have committed unto him against that day." Paul's confidence had nothing to do with himself. It was not because he thought he was smart or wise; it was not because he thought his way the best way. Paul did not compare himself with others. Paul had his confidence in Christ Jesus. His confidence in Christ Jesus was total, it was absolute. He absolutely believed that the death of Jesus Christ on Calvary's cross actually, really delivered him from sin, and that the resurrection of Jesus Christ from the dead actually, really opened the way for Paul to enter into the newness of life in Christ Jesus. He believed also that receiving the Holy Spirit was actually having the presence of God with him. Paul had committed his soul, his eternal future, to the living God. "That day" to which he referred is apparently the day of judgment. All human beings are expecting one way or another to come into the presence of God. Paul was satisfied that when he came into the presence of God the Lord Jesus Christ would be there to deliver him from the judgment. When the showdown came, Paul knew that he would go right on into glory. This was Paul's convinced assurance, on the basis of which he could in quietness and confidence go on with his ministry.

Chapter 4

PAUL'S FURTHER ADVICE TO TIMOTHY

After a person accepts Jesus Christ, what more should he do in order to have the blessing of God?

It is wonderful that the Gospel tells us salvation is of God. It is so comforting that God does for believers more than they can do for themselves. Believers can feel so blessed to think that He will carry them home. This has been a great comfort to my own heart and mind, but my natural inclination to laziness may lead me into error and loss. I can feel this when I read how Paul exhorts Timothy:

> Hold fast the form of sound words, which thou hast heard of me, in faith and love which is in Christ Jesus. That good thing which was committed unto thee keep by the Holy Ghost which dwelleth in us (2 Tim. 1:13-14).

It is true that believers in God trust in the Lord, and they are being saved because of this. But such believing is not done in a moment. It is much more than a matter of nodding one's head. A person does not yet believe because he finally agrees to say "yes." Believing means clinging to the Lord, holding to the Lord. The "form of sound words" are set forth in Scripture, in the Bible, but words are not all. It is the Spirit that giveth life. We understand that. But "sound words" guide the mind and the heart into the truth.

As you or I approach the Lord, when we turn our faces to God, and we want to think about God, we do not have to make up the truth. I often feel a certain sympathy when I hear some person, young or old, earnestly seeking to draw near to God, making up his own mind, making up his own heart. Of course one can appreciate his purpose, and I do not feel like condemning him, but I do wish he knew what to do.

There are true words which will actually guard your own heart and mind and lead them into the things of God. If you leave me to myself and I start talking, I hear my own words. The first thing you know, I will start believing what I am saying; so I say what I feel, and I go by that. But that is all coming out of me. And there is no guarantee for that. I do not naturally know the things of God. I cannot just reflect, sit back and think, and come out with the Word of God. That is not where it comes from. God must speak to me. He must show me. "Holy men of God spake as they were led by the Holy Spirit." Those words are "sound words." When I can get them into my mind, I can use them. They give me something to say that will be true and effectual.

Let us think about worshiping God. When you are thinking about turning to God in worship, you open your heart and mind, you look into His face, and you begin to talk. Has it ever occurred to you that you cannot say much? If I were to turn to God, lift up my heart and mind, look into His face and start talking of myself, there would not be much come out of me. But if I could remember the words of Scripture I could use them. For example, in worship, if I had my heart and mind filled with various expressions from the Psalms, the hymnbook of the Bible, they would lead me. "The Lord is my shepherd, I shall not want." What a wonderful idea! It was not mine; it was His. He gave it to me. Words used in the Bible are sound words. Words such as God, judgment, righteousness, sin, heaven, hell, salvation, being born again, angels, the devil, all these are sound words, true words. No one could condemn a person for using them. Timothy might not have had experience enough even in his honest sincere relationship with God to have language enough to know the deep important things of the Gospel, but Paul had had such experience. He was an older, more-experienced believer than Timothy, and as long as Timothy followed Paul's example he would be on the right track. But even in following Paul, Timothy is led to see that he, Timothy, must respond in Christ.

The true words that Paul would give to Timothy would lead Timothy into faith. Now faith is the one requirement for anybody who would be saved. It is "by grace that you are saved through faith and that not of yourselves, it is the gift of God."

Faith is that one requirement which everyone turning to the Lord must have. The believer will be led by the Holy Spirit in his heart to heed the Word of God. Believing the Word of God and obeying it—taking the Word of God, holding to the Word of God, the promises of God—is the way to God.

"Which thou hast heard of me, in faith and love" means Timothy is to hold fast the form of sound words in faith and love. "In faith" is his attitude toward God. "Love" could well be seen as his attitude toward man. The believer will be led by the Holy Spirit to love what God loves. The word "love" here is not so much a matter of sentiment as it is of preference. You will have to think that over. It is not how I feel; it is what I choose. As the believer is moved by the Holy Spirit he finds himself inclined to faith, which is about God.

"That good thing which was committed unto thee" probably was not any inward ability that Timothy had. This is not some personal grace given to Timothy in a special way. It more likely refers to his assignment. Timothy was given responsibility to take care of certain churches, and he was given the task of administering the Word of God to those churches. That was the good thing committed unto him. He was to "keep" it, that is guard, cherish, observe, and be careful in any kind of situation in which he might be. What is our responsibility? What is our part? What is lying at our feet to be done? We should be careful about it. You may have in mind to ask, "What do I have to do? The only thing I have is my house. The only thing to take care of is my family." All right, whatever it is, that is in your hand to do. Be careful about it. Observe its implications. Cherish that particular situation "by the Holy Ghost." How can one do this? Turn from self and yield to God.

For a moment let us pause here. When you say that you are going to keep something by the Holy Ghost, remember that no person should try to manipulate the Holy Spirit. The Holy Spirit is not someone that we can push around, or to Whom we can say, "Here, take care of this, or take care of that." The Holy Spirit in a certain sense is like the sun in the heavens. So far as the sun in the heavens is concerned, I can do nothing about it. I will tell you one thing I can do: I can turn my face up to the sun. I can walk out in the sun. When you say that I am to do something by the Holy Spirit, that does not mean that I use

Him. And yet I make use of Him. I put myself where He can work. The presence of the Holy Spirit is constant, so that any time I turn to face God, the Holy Spirit will show me the things of God. Diligence in remembering the presence of God is important for any believer.

Chapter 5

PAUL APPRECIATED PERSONAL SUPPORT

Do you realize that to help a witness of Christ in his testimony is to qualify for blessing from God?

The Gospel of Jesus Christ is carried to all men by witnesses for Christ. This is a simple fact. That is the way the Gospel spreads. A person who has been saved is now led by the Holy Spirit to tell other people about the Lord. He feels deep down in his own heart, "As my Father hath sent me, so send I you." And again he has heard a very plain word, "Go into all the world and preach the Gospel to every creature, making disciples of all nations." This command was given not to a special few, but to all believers.

Each believer has a responsibility to share in the joint operation of witnessing. We need to get the message out into the world that Christ Jesus came to seek and to save the lost. To fail to support this act of witnessing will incur wrath. This is not an elective that a believer can accept as he wishes; no, this is what we must do. In the Old Testament there was an occasion when the forces of Israel went up against an enemy. But some people did not help; and we have this hard word in the Old Testament Scriptures, found in Judges 5:23. "Curse ye Meroz, said the angel of the Lord, curse ye bitterly the inhabitants thereof; because they came not to the help of the Lord, to the help of the Lord against the mighty." That is a stern word! If I do not involve myself in sharing with those who are witnessing for the Gospel, I have to accept the consequences. God will not be pleased.

Now I am not commenting about unbelievers. I am sorry to say that unbelievers are lost. There is no point in pouring any more condemnation on them. It would be pouring water into a full cup. It could only overflow. But those of us who actually profess faith in the Lord Jesus Christ are inwardly led to do as He did. "As my Father hath sent me, so send I you." Going out into all the world and preaching the Gospel to every creature is my task, your task, every believer's task.

A particular incident in English history appealed to me as a boy and has appealed to me all my life. It occurred during the war that England had with Napoleon. Part of that war was fought at sea. At Cape Trafalgar a great naval victory was won by the English navy. The story goes that Admiral Lord Nelson, with a small fleet of relatively inferior ships, attacked the large fleet that Napoleon had amassed near Spain. When the day of the battle dawned, Lord Nelson put out on the flags of his flagship these famous words in English history: "England expects every man to do his duty." In Trafalgar Square in London, England, the memory of this whole incident is kept fresh in the minds of the English people and deeply etched into their hearts. I have felt many times that this is a proper way of saying I ought to respond when the Lord calls me to do His work.

Paul rates as a giant among witnesses, but Paul was conscious of those who were for him, those who did nothing, and those who were against him. Here are a few verses that bring all this to mind.

> This thou knowest, that all they which are in Asia be turned away from me; of whom are Phygellus and Hermogenes. The Lord give mercy unto the house of Onesiphorus; for he oft refreshed me, and was not ashamed of my chain: but, when he was in Rome, he sought me out very diligently, and found me. The Lord grant unto him that he may find mercy of the Lord in that day: and in how many things he ministered unto me at Ephesus, thou knowest very well (2 Tim. 1:15-18).

Did you notice he took note by name of those who turned away from him, and he took note of those who were for him? What a test it is to stand in a difficult place when people are walking away! What a strain it is to hold to a position when others turn their backs! Paul felt this, as any man would feel it. Your pastor will feel it. Your Sunday school teacher will feel it. The people who are working and serving in your church and in your community will feel it if you and I do not share with them and back them up. If they need means, we must give to them. If they need personal support, we must be there to support them. Our support is noticed here by those people, and I believe it is noted in heaven.

Then we read these wonderful words, "The Lord give mercy unto the house of Onesiphorus; for he oft refreshed me, and was not ashamed of my chain." Paul remembered with such deep gratitude that blessed man. "He stuck by me, and he came to make sure that I had what I needed. He would come to strengthen me. He was on my side. Even though they had me in jail, and I was being treated like a criminal, that man came and stood by me. He was not ashamed of my chain. But when he was in Rome he sought me out very diligently and found me. The Lord grant unto him that he may find mercy of the Lord in that day." I would love to find the mercy of the Lord in that day! Would not you love to find the mercy of the Lord in that day? What a simple way to qualify. Help the preacher, help the Sunday school teacher, help the fathers and mothers who are trying to bring up their children properly. Get into this whole business of witnessing for Christ if you are a believer.

These words were written to believers; do not misunderstand me. I think the common neglect on the part of all those that were in Asia served as a dark background to throw into bold relief the shining testimony of this man, Onesiphorus. I wish he had another name. If he could have a name something like ours, we would mention it more easily; but you know this man is worth thinking about. Here is a man that Paul marked out and said from the depth of his heart, "May God bless that man. When I was in a tight spot he stood by me." His claim to fame is that he went to great length to encourage and to support a preacher. It is God's Word we are declaring; it is God's Gospel we are sharing, and God knows it. Let us unite our hearts in a common obedience to the glory of God, and await His blessing.

Chapter 6

PAUL URGES TIMOTHY TO BE A GOOD SOLDIER

Can you see how a believer in Christ Jesus while living in this world under the guidance of the Holy Spirit is like a soldier under orders?

When Paul uses the figure of a soldier to refer to a believer, he is not primarily pointing to fighting the enemy, but to the soldier's relationship with his commanding officer and to his performance of routine duties. We will find this as we look in the second epistle of Paul to Timothy.

> Thou therefore, my son, be strong in the grace that is in Christ Jesus. And the things that thou hast heard of me among many witnesses, the same commit thou to faithful men, who shall be able to teach others also. Thou therefore endure hardness, as a good soldier of Jesus Christ. No man that warreth entangleth himself with the affairs of this life; that he may please him who hath chosen him to be a soldier. And if a man also strive for masteries, yet is he not crowned, except he strive lawfully (2 Tim. 2:1-5).

Paul was like a father to Timothy, that is to say, he showed Timothy certain truths and pointed out certain courses of action, watched over him while he was performing his work, noted his testimony, and guided him. So Paul spoke of him as "my son." He admonished him, "Be strong in the grace that is in Christ Jesus."

What gives a person a strong character or a strong personality? It is not the physical ability to do something heavy, not strong in a physical sense, but strong in the grace that is in Christ Jesus. But I raise the question, when is the person strong? I would say when he is persistent. That person is strong who not only has good ideas, but who sticks with them. Have you ever known in your own family circle some person who is a gentle, possibly a mild, perhaps even a timid person, who nonetheless is strong? When do you call him strong? Is it not true that you call him strong when he stands up under pressure, strong when you cannot shake him, strong when he never deviates? He goes right straight on through.

When a person is walking in the Lord, led by the Holy Spirit, he would be strong if he were continuously obedient. Not only on the nice days, not only on the downhill stretch, not only on smooth roads, but persistent all the way through, taking it as it comes, good and bad, up and down, quiet and boisterous, calm and stormy, never varying. That makes the person strong. You have accepted Christ, yielded yourself to Him, taken Him as your Lord and Savior, so now stick with Him all the way through. Paul will discuss that a little further.

Now notice that he says, "And the things that thou hast heard of me among many witnesses, the same commit thou to faithful men, who shall be able to teach others also." This was Timothy's particular task. This was what Timothy was to do. He was to take the message that he had received from Paul, the facts of the Gospel, and he was to share them with others so that they could, in turn, share them with still others. The Gospel is not a challenge for any human being to do something, and it is not advice on how to do things well, or how to do things wisely. Paul will tell you in First Corinthians 15:3-5 that Christ Jesus died for our sins according to the Scripture, that He was buried and that He arose again the third day according to the Scripture, and that He was seen. The witness should tell that. He should tell about the Lord Jesus Christ, not how pleasant He was, nor how kind He was, nor how gracious He was, nor how thoughtful He was, nor how wise He was. That would all be true, but that is not the Gospel. I am being rather specific here. The Gospel is that Christ died for my sins, was buried, that He arose from the dead for me, that He is in heaven now, and that He is coming again. Yes! That is the Gospel!

The Gospel is the statement of certain facts about Jesus Christ, some of which He has done, some of which He is doing, some of which He will do. Nobody on earth could guess it. Nobody on earth would have any idea if he were not told. Who should tell them? The people who have been told. It goes from telling to telling to telling. Paul had told Timothy the essence of the Gospel. Those facts of the Gospel needed to be shared with others if they were to believe and be saved. So Timothy was to commit these to faithful men. The word "faithful" does not mean trustworthy here so much as it means "believing" men. Tell this to believing men who shall be able to teach others if they believe, but the only way they can believe is if they know the facts. The witness who knows should share the facts.

"Thou therefore endure hardness, as a good soldier of Jesus Christ." The witness should take his share of the hardships that come, the sufferings that come. What would some of the sufferings be, some of the hardships be, that would come to the witness because he was a good soldier of Jesus Christ? It may happen that some people will be unkind to the witness, some people will persecute him. That might well be true, but it might not happen. That is really not the main problem for a good soldier of Christ.

What would some things be which would cause the witness to endure hardship? It may be that his personal desires will be denied. He may not be able to do as he pleases. He may not be able to get what he wants. He may have to give up certain personal ambitions. He must be meek at times of personal affront. Some people will not be friendly to him. Some people will insult him. Some people will just ignore him. If anyone has ever been through such experiences he will know this form of hardship. Under these circumstances it is hard to refrain from saying what could be said easily with such satisfaction. Another form of hardship is to have answers to prayer delayed, to keep praying with no answers. If the witness is to be a good soldier of Jesus Christ, he will need to stick with it. To be ridiculed or misrepresented because a person is a believer, while all the time he is carrying the load as a witness, is to endure hardness. The witness will put up with the things that happen to him because he is a good soldier of Jesus Christ.

Then Paul said something more: "No man that warreth entangleth himself with the affairs of this life; that he may please him who hath chosen him to be a soldier. And if a man also strive for masteries, yet is he not crowned, except he strive lawfully." The call to become a soldier is a demanding call. To become a good soldier of Jesus Christ is for the believer to hear the Holy Spirit from within calling him to take this stand: "This one thing I do." The believer is entitled to look ahead. He is encouraged to look ahead and expect the blessing of God which will be his to enjoy and will be his to share with others. That is what is going to happen as long as he walks with the Lord.

In all of this, we have implied several facts that you may have noticed. A believer can get entangled in the affairs of this life, which will distract him. These may be family matters, business matters, pleasure attractions, sports, amusements, or social relations. Time would run out to discuss all the various ways in which a person could get entangled. A soldier in the service should be kept free from such entanglements.

Paul then shifts the figure of speech for a soldier in the army to a contestant in the athletic field. "If a man also strive for masteries (if he is going to run a race and wants to win it), yet is he not crowned (he will not get the prize), except he strive lawfully." He will have to run that race according to regulations. No wonder we are able at times to sing with such appreciation,

"Take time to be holy, speak oft with thy Lord,
Abide in Him always, and feed on His Word.
Make friends of God's children, help those who are weak
Forgetting in nothing, His blessing to seek."

Sometime you should take that hymn and go through every stanza in it. It will guide you when you commit yourself to walk with the Lord, and be found with Him, all the way through, as a good soldier of Jesus Christ.

Chapter 7

THE PREACHER MUST PRACTICE WHAT HE PREACHES

Can you see that since the way of the cross leads home, the living experience of a believing person will include suffering?

The unique, special truth of the Gospel is that the soul is saved into eternal life by way of dying in the natural life to be resurrected in the spiritual life. This means that the course for any believer is actually a matter of dying to live. In this way he is translated out of the natural into the spiritual. I hope that this will not seem too strange for you. I suppose I should mention it more often because this is the way in which the blessing comes.

The Apostle Paul counted himself a master workman in this function of leading souls into the blessing of God. As a gardener labors to produce fruit in his garden, so Paul considered himself a husbandman who was laboring to bring souls into this blessing of God. Such ministry was not a matter of dictating things to be done. I know how commonly it is felt that preachers just preach, which is to say they keep telling you what you ought to do. But this is not the way it was with the Apostle Paul. For people who were already believers he told them what to do; but for people who did not know the Lord, Paul told them what the Lord had done. Actually, the ministry of Paul was performing the very process involved in ministering to others.

> The husbandman that laboureth must be first partaker of the fruits. Consider what I say; and the Lord give thee understanding in all things. Remember that Jesus Christ of the seed of David was raised from the dead according to my gospel: wherein I suffer trouble, as an evil doer, even unto bonds; but the word of God is not bound. Therefore I endure all things for the elect's sake, that they may also obtain the salvation which is in Christ Jesus with eternal glory (2 Tim. 2:6-10).

The Preacher Must Practice What He Preaches 135

Here Paul states the basic operative principle, the basic way in which things are done. Even as Christ Jesus gave Himself to die, to be buried, to be raised from the dead, so must the minister of the Gospel give himself as a pilot demonstration. He must show how it is done. Not only must he show how it is done, but he needs to do it that others might be led this way. If a witness for Christ wants to be effectual in bringing souls to life in God, he must himself first experience the Gospel in coming to God. In other words, the man who is going to preach the Gospel of Jesus Christ, pointing out how a person can move from the natural into the spiritual, must himself die in the natural, be buried, and be raised in the spiritual. This is implied in a well-known Scripture: "The husbandman that laboureth must be first partaker of the fruits."

For many years I thought this Scripture verse was a way of indicating that the pastor should get his salary. Now I realize that is not what it means at all. What it means is that the person who is leading other people into spiritual life must himself first of all move into spiritual life. The fruits to which he refers are not salary, wages. The fruits are love, joy, peace, longsuffering, goodness, gentleness, self-control, and faith. What Paul is here telling this young preacher is that if Timothy is going to lead other people into this kind of blessing, he must have it first. He must first be a partaker of these things before he can share them with other people.

And this is why Paul calls on Timothy to endure hardness, as a good soldier of Jesus Christ. What kind of hardness? Suffering, self-denial, self-crucifixion. He called upon Timothy to do this that he might be wholly committed as a good soldier. He was going to have to die in the flesh and be raised in the Spirit, so that he might lead others to die in the flesh that they might be raised in the Spirit. If he were going to be the leader he would have to walk in front of them. If he were going to bring them into spiritual life, he needed to be in spiritual life.

I expect what I am emphasizing here is this idea that the preacher does not just tell people what to do. He personally experiences and thus ministers the Gospel, leading others into it. I am referring to a preacher because Timothy and Paul were preachers. But this principle also applies to parents. If I am going to lead my boy to a fellowship with God, I must myself be in fellowship with God. If I try to stand behind him and push him, he will not go; but if I lead him he might come. The mother who is going to lead her child into spiritual blessing must herself personally be in spiritual blessing. The husbandman and the gardener, the person who is producing the fruit, must be the first partaker; he must first do these things himself.

The very essence of the message is expressed in verse 8: "Remember that Jesus Christ of the seed of David was raised from the dead according to my gospel." That is the whole point. Hearing the Gospel is hearing what ought to happen inside my soul, inside your soul, hearing what ought to happen in us, by the power of God and the grace of God working in us. The very essence of what I am preaching is that Jesus Christ Himself was raised from the dead. To die, to be buried, to be resurrected in the newness of life is the royal way of living. That is the way it is done.

Paul was an example as he wrote in verse 9: "Wherein I suffer trouble, as an evil doer, even unto bonds; but the word of God is not bound." Paul suffered, but the Word of God moved on. He had troubles, but the Word of God moved in other people. He was even in prison and in danger of death, but his preaching was effective. They put him in jail, but the Word of God was never hindered because by that means it was being put forward. Paul could say: "Therefore I endure all things." I think Paul meant to say, "I endure them willingly. I am willing to have these things happen to me. I endure all things for the elect's sake," for the sake of those people who have been called in the Gospel to put their trust in the Lord Jesus Christ. "That they may also obtain the salvation which is in Christ Jesus." In order that those people listening to Paul could understand what was actually true, Paul himself went through the experience of dying, being buried as it were, and being raised from the dead unto eternal life, all to the praise and glory of the Savior.

As a witness, following Paul's example, Timothy too could minister the Gospel to others, leading souls through the process of dying into the blessedness of living. But the only way that Timothy could do that was for himself to go through that first.

Chapter 8

THE ISSUE OF THE GOSPEL IS SIMPLE

Can you see that being honest or sincere is not enough to qualify for receiving a blessing? Can you understand how a person might be honest and sincere, and yet fail?

I grew up on a farm, and farmers deal with nature directly. There are some good farmers and some poor farmers. The good farmers are those who know how to adjust themselves to the laws of nature in such a way that they have good crops. That has no bearing at all on what kind of a man is running the machines. It has no bearing at all on whether he is an honest man or a crook, whether he is sincere or whether he is a liar. If he works the land properly he will get a good crop. If he does not work the land properly he will not get a good crop.

This truth can be seen in other things as well. A man who is a crook might drive on the highway carefully, obeying the laws of traffic, and he might go a long way before he has any trouble. Another man driving on the highway might be an honest man, a sincere man, who may even be engaged in a mission of righteousness; but if he drives carelessly and is thoughtless about what he is doing, he is liable to have a wreck. That wreck will be because of how he drove, not because of what kind of man he is. The truth is like that.

It is not enough that a mechanic should be honest. It would be a fine thing if he were, but that is not enough. He needs to know about cars if he is going to make a success of repairing cars. It is not enough for the gardener to be a truthful man with integrity. He needs to know how to plant beans if he wants to get beans. And it is not enough for a preacher to be humble and sincere; he needs to know what is in the Bible and how to get it across.

Fortunately knowledge can be learned. A believer can read the Bible, listen to what it says, and study to see how he can put together what it is saying. He can know what he needs to know. Some persons in the congregation are called gifts of God to the church. Some are able to hear clearly, understand plainly, then say it simply; and they are a marvelous help to other people. They understand the meaning of Scripture, and they can talk about it and explain it to other people. Some persons are gifted for such services, and God helps some to be more gifted than others. In His own wisdom He gave some to be pastors, some to be evangelists, some to be teachers. They help others to believe, they help others to understand, and they help others to grow.

Paul was such a person, and he understood about himself. He taught the meaning of the Gospel to other believers. What is in the Gospel does not come to anyone out of the clear air. "Faith cometh by hearing and hearing by the Word of God." Paul pointed out how this works.

> It is a faithful saying: For if we be dead with him, we shall also live with him: if we suffer, we shall also reign with him: if we deny him, he also will deny us: if we believe not, yet he abideth faithful: he cannot deny himself. Of these things put them in remembrance, charging them before the Lord that they strive not about words to no profit, but to the subverting of the hearers (2 Tim. 2:11-14).

The call into spiritual life is by way of dying unto self and living unto God. The call is to go through death into eternal life. Paul told Timothy that if we have yielded ourselves into His death, "we shall also live with him." The wonderful thing about that is while I may need to commit myself to die, I do not have to arouse myself to get up from the dead. If I yield myself to God He will raise me from the dead. If I yield myself to God in any given situation and simply let Him work out His will, He will make out of me something I was not before. It will be better with me because of what God does.

"If we suffer, we shall also reign with him." That is the same principle: we die to live. In this world you will have tribulations; in that world you will have glory. The route is from here to there. Now we are in trouble; then we are in glory. Now we suffer; then we are on the throne with Him. "If we suffer, we shall also reign with him: if we deny him, he also will deny us."

The Issue of the Gospel Is Simple 139

A person should not complain about that. This whole truth is shaped this way and put this way so that human beings will come to realize there is cause and effect involved. If we want certain good results, we will do some things that we are led to do. They will hurt us now, but we will be better off then. That is about the way it is.

Paul then pointed out something that is different. "If we believe not, yet he abideth faithful." Notice the rhythm of these sentences. "If we be dead with him, we shall also live with him; if we suffer, we shall also reign with him; if we deny him, he also will deny us; if we believe not, yet he abideth faithful." Paul does not say "If we believe not, He will not believe either." At this point Paul breaks his rhythm to say that "If we believe not, yet He abideth faithful: He cannot deny Himself." This is one of the most wonderful thoughts to give a person confidence before God. It is not so much that I turn to God, put my trust in Him, and lay hold on Him, but God comes to me, lays His hold on me. It is God's hold on me that will save my soul. I might give out and not have the strength. He has, and my salvation is safe and secure because God is going to hold me. I turn to Him, I raise my hand to Him, lay my hand in His, and grip it the best I can, but I do not have the strength. I am not strong enough, faithful enough; I might even give up. But when once He takes hold of me, "He that hath begun a good work in you will complete it."

"Of these things put them in remembrance." This was Timothy's job. Tell the people. Get it across to them. "Charging them before the Lord that they strive not about words to no profit, but to the subverting of the hearers." This brings to our mind immediately one of the greatest snares of all Bible study, Bible conferences, and Bible teaching: people can argue about the meaning of a word, and immediately others feel that there is a great difference between the two meanings. The Bible does not bear out this conclusion. One snare we must avoid is arguing the exact meaning of the words used. Such arguments are useless. They have a bad negative effect. Sometimes a Bible teacher may not hold a straight course through the truth because he is interested in his own ideas. And yet it would not be wise to engage him in controversy at the point where he began to follow his own ideas.

Chapter 9

PAUL'S ADVICE TO BELIEVERS

Since God chooses His servants in His own sovereign wisdom, is there anything a believer might do to qualify as a special servant of God?

> Study to show thyself approved unto God, a workman that needeth not to be ashamed, rightly dividing the word of truth. But shun profane and vain babblings: for they will increase unto more ungodliness. And their word will eat as doth a canker: of whom is Hymenaeus and Philetus; who concerning the truth have erred, saying that the resurrection is past already; and overthrow the faith of some. Nevertheless the foundation of God standeth sure, having this seal, The Lord knoweth them that are his. And, Let every one that nameth the name of Christ depart from iniquity (2 Tim. 2:15-19).

Preachers should be diligent in studying the Bible so they will know how to lead others in a clear way. But when I have said that about preachers, I have not only said what is true for preachers, but what is also true for parents. We who believe in the Lord Jesus Christ and have families want them to believe in the Lord Jesus Chirst. We did not pick up our faith from the world. It came to us in a spiritual fashion, and in one way or another was basically centered in the Scriptures and what we understood about Jesus Christ. The world does not tell us about Jesus Christ. People in the world have ideas about Him, but their ideas are not based on facts.

The facts about the Lord Jesus Christ are in Scripture, and so not only should preachers study the Bible, but parents also should get to know the Bible. Sunday school teachers should study the Bible, as should all believing people, especially those who want to help others. For a preacher to be ignorant of the Bible, of the Scriptures, about salvation, Paul would say that is a shame. If a believer who has a family does not get to know what is actually involved in accepting Christ and walking with Him, it is really a shame.

Knowing the Scriptures is not a matter of remembering the words that are used. You do not really get to know the Bible by memorizing it, although that is a wonderful help. It is a matter of knowing how the words of God lead the soul. When Paul told Timothy that he wanted him to study, to show himself approved unto God, "a workman that needeth not to be ashamed, rightly dividing the word of truth," you should understand that he means "as a ship ploughs through the waves of the sea." The ship sails straight ahead, no matter which way the waves are running, and holds a straight course. One translator put it this way, "ploughing a straight furrow." Another one in a more general way says, "correctly interpreting the Word." How do I know what any passage in the Bible means? Because I know the other passages in the Bible. No single Scripture standing by itself can be adequately interpreted. The Bible needs to be understood in the light of what the whole Bible says. The Word of God leads the believer into total commitment to God.

"But shun profane and vain babblings: for they will increase unto more ungodliness." The word "profane" refers to the person who talks about the things of God as if they were merely ordinary, or the person who talks about spiritual experiences as if they were simply human affairs. That makes their comments profane. The believer is to "shun" such things so that he does not get into arguments like that. "Vain babblings," empty talk, does not need any description. We know what that means.

Paul wrote to Timothy, "Don't get into that kind of argument. Stay away from those useless things. For they will increase unto more ungodliness." Arguing about religion actually results in people being worse than they were before. "And their word will eat as doth a canker." You and I would say "cancer." "Their word," that kind of argument, that kind of talk, that kind of idea will just eat inside your heart and mind like cancer in your body. You read, for example, about the virgin birth, and then you argue with persons who do not believe it. You read about the Lord Jesus walking on the water, and some will say, "I don't think it really happened that way." You read in the book of Acts about the prison gates being opened and Peter and John coming out, and then you discuss this with persons who deep down in their hearts think, "That sounds all right, but I don't think it really happened that way." If you start arguing about any one of those ideas in any one of those passages, the effect will go through your whole consciousness, and it will ruin your whole conception of Christ. It will eat in you like a cancer eats in the body. That is what will happen. If you have an article of clothing that is knit, you know that when you pull a thread, you pull and pull the thread, and as you pull the thread you are undoing the whole fabric.

Do you follow me? If a question is raised about something that is in Scripture, when you were not there to actually see the event, the man talking to you was not there, and none of the people in the discussion were present at the time; then each starts putting his own mind to these Scriptures and argues and discusses and raises questions, and that goes on and on. The first thing you know your whole conception of the Bible is ruined.

That is what Paul means when he says, "And their word will eat as doth a canker: of whom is Hymenaeus and Philetus; who concerning the truth have erred, saying that the Resurrection is past already; and overthrow the faith of some." How would they say the Resurrection is past already? Such persons might feel that emphasizing the Resurrection of the Lord Jesus Christ is what the whole Gospel is about. The body of Jesus Christ was raised, but if you stop considering the idea of Resurrection at that point, you will miss out for yourself. Actually the Resurrection of the body of the Lord Jesus Christ teaches me and you not only that one day in the future our bodies will be raised from the dead, but while we are here, we can live in Resurrection life. Paul is anxious to emphasize that this whole truth of the Resurrection is a current truth. It is happening right now. So he said that when these people say the Resurrection is past already, they overthrow the faith of some.

"Nevertheless the foundation of God standeth sure, having this seal." After this you will read two statements: "The Lord knoweth them that are his. And, let every one that nameth the name of Christ depart from iniquity." A seal was like a medal. It was like a coin that you see people carry sometimes. On one side is printed, "The Lord knows them that are His," and on the other side is printed, "Let every one that nameth the name of Christ depart from iniquity." Paul says this is absolutely sure. We should not let anybody shake us away from these things. The Lord knows them that are His, meaning to say, the Lord has communion, fellowship; and He actually associates with those that are His. Believers should have godly conduct. Communion with the Lord and godly conduct are in the very heart of the Christian Gospel.

Here we see how Paul answers the whole question about the error of saying the Resurrection is past already. He does not argue that. He does not bring any other Scripture to bear on that. He simply calls upon Timothy to emphasize to the people that performance counts. Communion with God, godly conduct in the world, is the very essence of responding to the Lord Jesus Christ.

Chapter 10

THE FAITHFUL WITNESS MUST BE CAREFUL IN HIS CONDUCT

Can you understand why a minister of the Gospel, as a servant of the Lord, should never argue?

> But in a great house there are not only vessels of gold and of silver, but also of wood and of earth; and some to honour, and some to dishonour. If a man therefore purge himself from these, he shall be a vessel unto honour, sanctified, and meet for the master's use, and prepared unto every good work. Flee also youthful lusts: but follow righteousness, faith, charity, peace, with them that call on the Lord out of a pure heart. But foolish and unlearned questions avoid, knowing that they do gender strifes. And the servant of the Lord must not strive; but be gentle unto all men, apt to teach, patient, in meekness instructing those that oppose themselves; if God peradventure will give them repentance to the acknowledging of the truth; and that they may recover themselves out of the snare of the devil, who are taken captive by him at his will (2 Tim. 2:20-26).

Another translation reads, beginning with verse 20, "But in a great house there are not only vessels of gold and silver but also (utensils) of wood and earthenware, and some for honorable and noble (use) and some for menial and ignoble (use.) So whoever cleanses himself (from what is ignoble and unclean)—who separates himself from contact with contaminating and corrupting influences—will (then himself) be a vessel set apart and useful for honorable and noble purposes, consecrated and profitable to the Master, fit and ready for any good work." A person who is going to speak for the Lord should be careful not to speak of other things too much. Certainly there are other things that are helpful.

I remember some years ago people would ask me questions about the affairs of my native country, Canada, and about the British Empire. I would talk about these things, and the time

The Faithful Witness Must Be Careful in His Conduct 145

would pass interestingly enough. This happened off and on from time to time for several years, but I began to feel it was not good. I could have been talking about missions. I could have been talking about the spreading of the Gospel. There were various things that I could have discussed apart from spending my time in what actually amounted to vain and empty discussion. I have always appreciated the privilege of declaring the Gospel, and the benefits of having a voice that can be heard, and having a mind that can think on these things; and I have sought to prove worthy of revelation from God that I can share with other people. This has resulted in my making it a principle that I do not appear in public to speak about anything except the name of the Lord Jesus Christ. In referring to this experience of mine, I am only illustrating what it means for a man who is a witness for the Lord, who accepts responsibility, to see to it that his public stance, his public address, his public image, is committed to the Person of the Lord Jesus Christ. This is what Paul wanted Timothy to have.

Now let us read on and see what he wrote further than this. "Flee also youthful lusts: but follow righteousness, faith, charity, peace, with them that call on the Lord out of a pure heart." This word "lust" must be understood to mean only "strong desires." Of course there are times when such lead to evil. This is just in the course of nature. But the words "youthful lusts" as they are used here in the New Testament simply mean "strong desires of youth." Paul told Timothy to get away from those.

Timothy was a young man, and Paul told this young man to be careful not to fall into the usual allurements, the usual interests that young people have. This is very striking, and we ask ourselves: "Does this mean a young person is not yet ready to serve the Lord?" Oh, no. It only means that any young person must be very careful to remember that he is young. While I am noting that, I would like to put in on the other hand that the old person should be careful to avoid those things that go with age. Because, just as it is true that young people can be moved by strong desires of youth, it is also true that often old people take advantage of their age.

Paul wrote that as a witness for the Lord Jesus Christ Timothy should humbly, simply follow the Lord. "But follow righteousness, faith, charity, peace." These traits are right down the middle of the road. Righteousness has to do with conduct, faith has to do with the Scriptures, charity has to do with other people, with love toward the poor, and peace with all men. The meaning of those words "pure heart" can be felt in the word "purified." That is the only way human hearts will ever be pure. So Paul asked Timothy to be careful to avoid falling into natural snares of any kind, but to commit himself definitely to the pursuit of righteousness. This word "follow" really means to "chase after," like a boy running to catch onto the rear end of a truck to get a ride.

"Follow righteousness, faith, charity, peace, with them that call on the Lord out of a pure heart. But foolish and unlearned questions avoid, knowing that they do gender strifes." Here was another clear word to this young preacher. Timothy was not to get into foolish and unlearned questions, such as are not based on a knowledge of the Scriptures. People who do not know what the Bible actually has in it will start arguing about the Bible. As long as they do not know the Scriptures, how can anyone help them in any very definite way? The young witness should avoid foolish and unlearned questions.

Another translation renders this passage thus: "But refuse—shut your mind against, have nothing to do with—trifling (ill-informed, unedifying, stupid) controversies over ignorant questionings, for you know that they foster strife and breed quarrels."

Yet another scholar translates more simply and more quietly with words like this: "Again I say, don't get involved in foolish arguments which only upset people and make them angry."

And another writes: "Have nothing to do with stupid, senseless controversies; you know that they breed quarrels."

The next verses bring out more clearly this emphasis. "And the servant of the Lord must not strive; but be gentle unto all men, apt to teach, patient, in meekness instructing those that oppose themselves; if God peradventure will give them repentance to the acknowledging of the truth; and that they may recover themselves out of the snare of the devil, who are taken captive by him at his will." This is a very serious assignment. The servant of the Lord must not strive, engage in no quarreling at all, but be gentle unto all men. That is a real task.

It is easy to be gentle to gentle people, such as a child, an infant, the sick; but to be gentle unto all men! "Apt to teach" means ready, equipped, and able to tell the other person what he needs to know. "Patient" means persistent, to stay with it, to "hang in there." "In meekness instructing those that oppose themselves." Meekness is suffering personal indignity. What all this means is that when people despise you, Paul would say, "Be meek, don't fight back. Just have it understood that you are never going to defend yourself."

The witness should do this with reference to all people, "instructing those that oppose themselves." There are some people whose personal procedure is not even good for themselves. Their conduct actually hurts them. That kind of people, people who are acting to their own hurt, are folks who need help and the witness of the Gospel. Some of them are ensnared. They do not really want to do what they do, but they act as they do because they are caught in something they cannot control. The witness should be kind to those people; he should be meek in the presence of those people: "That they may recover themselves." We should notice that this is the only way those folks will ever be free. No outsider can deliver them from the snare of the devil. They got in of their own free will and accord, and they are going to get out that way. The Lord will call them, and energize them, and strengthen them, but the witness must keep his testimony so that they may recover themselves out of the snare of the devil.

Chapter 11

SIN WILL GROW WORSE AND WORSE

Do you realize that the Scriptures reveal that God, in His foreknowledge, expected widespread moral decay?

> This know also, that in the last days perilous times shall come. For men shall be lovers of their own selves, covetous, boasters, proud, blasphemers, disobedient to parents, unthankful, unholy, without natural affection, trucebreakers, false accusers, incontinent, fierce, despisers of those that are good, traitors, heady, highminded, lovers of pleasures more than lovers of God (2 Tim. 3:1-4).

Anyone reading the New Testament would know that men of God expected that moral conditions in the world would go from bad to worse. This is brought out especially clearly in this statement by the Apostle Paul. This Scripture is a serious, sober catalog of vices and of traits of character that are degenerative. You cannot say too much against this kind of thing, and yet it is very common. Paul gave Timothy to understand this is the way things would be, generally speaking.

By the way, that does not mean that each of these traits were possessed by this many separate individual persons. This was the general mood, the general frame of mind, the general type of character that would be found among people. You could probably find some one person who would exhibit three or four or five of these traits, because they all belong together.

Conduct, anybody's conduct, is the responsibility of that individual. But that conduct is often influenced by others. I have often thought in that respect about something in the natural world. I am sure you have often seen, either directly or in a picture, a stream of water flowing rapidly down a mountainside. Oftentimes it is very thrilling to see. Then again you might see a stream of water flowing sluggishly along in a meadow, winding in and out, so quietly and so smoothly you can hardly see it moving. It is the same water. Now let me emphasize that again. It is the same water. The water itself does not make it jump over stones, and the water does not make it go quietly and smoothly in the meadow. It is the environment, we would say the terrain, the slope of the land, that makes the water lie quietly in a pool or dash over rocks in rapids. It is the same water.

There is something in this that is suggestive of us human beings. Human beings do not act the same in every situation. Remember the old saying, "A man is known by the company he keeps," or "Birds of a feather flock together." We are affected by the folks with whom we associate. One reason we keep the company we do is these people are the folks we like. But so far as the public is concerned, we can have one thing in mind: we cannot escape them. You and I have to live among them, and according to the way they act, we are affected.

This is what causes us to say humbly that it is a wonderful blessing to belong to a praying church. I mean a congregation that gets together and prays openly. It is a wonderful thing to be in the presence of praying people, within earshot of praying people, so that you can hear folks pray. That is marvelous because it influences you and encourages you.

Paul warns Timothy of dangerous conditions that will develop in the future. Paul was writing to Timothy many hundreds of years ago, but this prospect is true even to this day. When Paul wrote "in the last days" it is not clear just what he meant. Many people feel that the phrase "the last days" should refer to the last little while before Christ returns. But Scripture seems to discourage us from thinking about that.

> And he said unto them, It is not for you to know the times or the seasons, which the Father hath put in his own power (Acts 1:7).

Then what could be the last days? From the time Jesus Christ ascended into heaven until the time that He comes again, so far as God's whole overall program from creation to the end of the world is concerned, this could be the "last" period. There is not anything else coming after this but the end. In that sense it is the last.

"In the last days perilous times shall come." In what sense perilous? Dangerous, because of public customs and attitudes.

The description is general. When everybody is careless, it is easy to be careless. When everybody forgets things, it is easy to be forgetful. Anyone is influenced by others. If everybody is shouting, you can tend to be loud. If everybody talks quietly, your voice drops. We are affected by people. This is how another scholar translated this passage.

> You may as well know this too, Timothy, that in the last days it is going to be very difficult to be a Christian. For people will love only themselves and their money; they will be proud and boastful, sneering at God, disobedient to their parents, ungrateful to them, and thoroughly bad. They will be hardheaded and never give in to others; they will be constant liars and troublemakers and will think nothing of immorality. They will be rough and cruel, and sneer at those who try to be good. They will betray their friends; they will be hotheaded, puffed up with pride, and prefer good times to worshiping God (2 Tim. 3:1-4).

I do not know when the end of time will come, but these conditions seem to exist here now.

The rest of the chapter continues with Paul's personal word to Timothy. The words of Paul give a clue to believers as to what they might do in this time. His whole message comes down to where he said to Timothy:

> Preach the word; be instant in season, out of season; reprove, rebuke, exhort with all long-suffering and doctrine. For the time will come when they will not endure sound doctrine; but after their own lusts shall they heap to themselves teachers, having itching ears (2 Tim. 4:2-3).

Chapter 12

THE WEAKNESS OF PRETENSE

Can you see how pretending to be good results in barren living?

> Having a form of godliness, but denying the power thereof: from such turn away. For of this sort are they which creep into houses, and lead captive silly women laden with sins, led away with divers lusts, ever learning, and never able to come to the knowledge of the truth (2 Tim. 3:5-7).

Tying apples to a cedar tree does not make it an apple tree. That may seem to be a silly idea, but it applies to what we are studying, living by faith in Christ. Perhaps there is no saying of Paul that is more cutting or sinister than this which Paul wrote about certain people: "Having a form of godliness, but denying the power thereof." "Form" means the outward appearance. Paul referred to certain persons who had the outward appearance of godliness, when actually their performance did not bear out their claim of belonging to Christ. They said they believed, but they never acted that way. At another time Paul wrote:

> They profess that they know God; but in works they deny him, being abominable, and disobedient, and unto every good work reprobate (Titus 1:16).

We pause and ask ourselves, who would such people be? Would there be any around us today who have a form of godliness but deny the power thereof? Let me offer some suggestions. How about those people who join the church and then never come to share in the life of the church? Or what shall we say about persons who claim publicly that they believe the Bible. But they never read it, never study it, so they do not obey it, do not try to find out about it. They say they believe it and then leave it closed. Is that not having a form of godliness and denying the power, not letting it work in you? Or consider persons who say they believe in prayer and then never pray. They say they believe in prayer, but they never go to prayer meeting. Or take for instance people who say they believe in missions. They are inclined to honor missionaries, and if you had a special missionary gathering at your church they would come and they would feel very kindly about those missionaries. But they never give, and they never pray for those missionaries. Now they profess, they have a form of godliness, but they never perform. Thus they deny the power thereof.

When we come to more spiritual matters, we have people who claim to have the Holy Spirit. They understand about the doctrine enough to know that God has given the Holy Spirit to every believer, so they say they have the Holy Spirit. Who is going to deny it? Who is going to challenge them? For myself I can just look in the mirror. I will look at myself and ask myself, "If I do have the Holy Spirit in me, is there love in my heart? Do I care about people? Do I want to help people? Am I actually concerned about unbelievers? Does it bother me about those who walk away from God?" And then again, if I say I have the Holy Spirit, do I have joy? That is one of the gifts along with love and peace. Can I honestly, truthfully say that deep down in my heart I am glad in the presence of God? Then again they say they have the Holy Spirit but they have no peace. They are troubled. They are burdened. They are concerned. They are under strain. Now I do not want to be unkind, I know I am probing about different things, but honestly this bothers me, "having a form of godliness but denying the power thereof."

If I turn up the furnace, there should be some heat coming forth. If I get into the car and step on the starter, it is supposed to turn. If I put my foot on the gas, the engine is supposed to run. If these things do not happen, what then? Something is wrong. This is what I have been trying to bring out, and this is what Paul pointed out. In the opening verses Paul alerted Timothy to these people. They were folks who love themselves, indulge themselves, who are lovers of pleasure more than lovers of God. Mind you, these people were right there among the apostles.

The Weakness of Pretense

What was Timothy to do? Expose them, such as I have been doing? But I am not talking out loud, and I do not point out individuals. In any case, what should a man do? What should Timothy do? Should he exhort them? Should he admonish them? Or perhaps somebody will say, "He can pray for them." I do not want to be unkind about that, but let me point out what Paul would do. Avoid them. Such people are afflicted by secret sins. Timothy should get away from them.

"Having a form of godliness, but denying the power thereof: from such turn away. For of this sort are they which creep into houses, and lead captive silly women laden with sins, led away with divers lusts, ever learning, and never able to come to the knowledge of the truth." What a picture this is of our secular campuses today, and what a tragedy! Persons are trying to find out, some going this way, some going that way. They make a big show of the fact that they are hunting truth. What a snare this is that threatens souls! They make a bold proclamation of a high noble purpose. They attract earnest souls who will spend themselves and all they have to achieve this goal. But they are doomed to failure, because they have not gone the way the Lord wanted them to go.

It is not what we profess; it is how we deny ourselves. It is not what we claim; it is how we yield. It is not what we say; it is what we do. We can always remember that a humble and a contrite heart the Lord will not despise. If we humbly, earnestly, sincerely turn to God and put ourselves before Him and thrust ourselves upon His mercy, God will save to the uttermost those who come unto Him through the Lord Jesus Christ. We thank God for this and pray His blessing upon us as we think on these things.

Chapter 13

OPPONENTS OF THE GOSPEL

Can you understand why a person telling the truth about God would be opposed?

The common experience of any witness for Christ who will talk up in favor of Jesus Christ is to be opposed, to be persecuted. One could very well ask, "Why?" It often happens that these people who talk about the Lord Jesus Christ are really kind people, gracious, and helpful to others. If you stop to think about it, those people who will talk about the Lord and who will pray to God are actually those among us who will be doing varied helpful things in the community. Why then is there such opposition, and why would there be such persecution which shows up in various ways?

You and I should never forget the reality of the devil, the deadly hostility of Satan. We ought to know right now that if we name the name of Christ Jesus, Satan is opposed to us. We can also have in mind the bad conscience of people who know that they are in the wrong, and if we even mention the name of God they feel smitten. If we mention the name of the Lord Jesus Christ, they feel they have left something out, which is true. But it brings it to their minds, and they wish we would just hush and keep quiet.

The basic thrust of the Gospel is to deny self. The Gospel calls upon anybody and everybody to deny himself. People do not want to hear that. They are doing what they like to do. Of course they are indulging themselves, but they like to do it. If anyone mentions the things of Christ and talks about prayer, immediately they feel that speaker is putting limitations on them, and he is trying to restrict them. Among other things, in

Opponents of the Gospel 155

a different way, there is offended pride. Human beings would like to think that if they ever do anything good, that should be to their credit. But the truth is that everything comes from the Lord Jesus Christ. This offends the pride of some people. This is how Paul explained it to Timothy:

> Now as Jannes and Jambres withstood Moses, so do these also resist the truth: men of corrupt minds, reprobate concerning the faith. But they shall proceed no further: for their folly shall be manifest unto all men, as theirs also was (2 Tim. 3:8-9).

In these verses Paul recalls that when Moses was contending with Pharaoh about having the children of Israel released from bondage in that country, there were certain men who opposed Moses before Pharaoh. They were called the magicians. They encouraged Pharaoh to resist Moses' request. When Moses performed certain miracles, these magicians did similar feats. When we see the word "magician" we probably think of somebody in a long-tailed coat and a top hat doing "miracles," pulling rabbits out of hats or drawing a flag out of an empty space, or something like that. We are inclined to think of the kind of magician that puts on parlor tricks. That is not what these men were. This word "magician" in the Old Testament was the only word that they had for our word "scientist."

Science and magic are very much alike. You see, magic is a procedure by which a person tries to control events, and science is a procedure by which a person would like to control events. The difference between magic and science is not in the purpose, but in the procedure. In the case of magic there is no practical relation between the means and end. Does that sound obscure to you? How is carrying a rabbit foot in your pocket going to give you a safe trip? The rabbit's foot does not have anything to do with it. What about carrying a four leaf clover to give you good luck? The four leaf clover would not have anything to do with it.

By way of contrast, how would science work? This is how science would work. On a particular road you should not drive more than 50 miles an hour. Then you would stay on the road safely, and you would not need any rabbit's foot or four leaf clover. The magicians were men who manipulated events. They were able to manipulate things in such a way that they produced the same results that Moses did. Now Paul tells Timothy that just as there were men who opposed Moses, so there will be men opposing the Gospel today.

How then shall a witness proceed? The one sure factor that promises victory at a time of such opposition is personal testimony. Notice what Paul says at this point when he goes on writing to Timothy. In the face of any and all opposition he tells Timothy this:

> But thou hast fully known my doctrine, manner of life, purpose, faith, longsuffering, charity, patience, persecutions, afflictions, which came unto me at Antioch, at Iconium, at Lystra; what persecutions I endured: but out of them all the Lord delivered me (2 Tim. 3:10-11).

Notice the succession of those items. First he mentions doctrine. This is what he was there for; he was teaching the Gospel. Then he mentions manner of life. This is part of the witnessing that is done for others. The way the witness lives actually affects people's hearts and minds. Now we should notice the next item, his purpose. The thrust of his activity was definite. Paul's doctrine and his manner of life had a purpose. He wanted to do something about it all. He wanted his hearers to know that Jesus Christ was the Savior and Lord. Faith was basic to all that he taught, to all that he did, to all that he aimed at. Deep down in his heart he accepted the revelation of God as true and went by that.

Long-suffering is having faith, and going through with teaching and living and following the Christian life, as Timothy was doing. He would have opposition. But long-suffering means persistence in the face of opposition. Paul did not quit. It is interesting to see that charity comes right after long-suffering. This is the way it happens: a person needs charity when he has been in trouble. When someone else is troubling the witness, and then he is gracious to that troubler, this is really the grace of God. This means that he had charity in spite of his own suffering. Patience is endurance in spite of long delay. Persecution is when others poured their opposition onto the witness. Affliction is the actual distress that the witness suffered. As we look through those words we find one follows another, one growing out of the other. Does anyone ever forget opposition? Not so much; but one forgives it. And this is what Paul did. How did Paul respond to his opposition? He endured. Why was he not blotted out? Why was he not overcome? Can any human being overcome God's people? "Out of them all the Lord delivered me."

Chapter 14

TIMOTHY'S FORTUNATE CHILDHOOD

Do you realize the importance of teaching the Gospel to children?

Timothy was the most prominent helper Paul had in all his Gospel labors. Paul could say about Timothy words like this, "I have no man like-minded who will naturally care for your state." There is no account of Timothy passing through anything like conversion, but Paul writes this about him in the first chapter of Second Timothy: "When I call to remembrance the unfeigned faith that is in thee, which dwelt first in thy grandmother Lois, and thy mother Eunice; and I am persuaded that in thee also." Now in the passage before us we have words from Paul that describe Timothy's experience even more fully.

> Yea, and all that will live godly in Christ Jesus shall suffer persecution. But evil men and seducers shall wax worse and worse, deceiving, and being deceived. But continue thou in the things which thou hast learned and hast been assured of, knowing of whom thou hast learned them; and that from a child thou hast known the holy scriptures, which are able to make thee wise unto salvation through faith, which is in Christ Jesus (2 Tim. 3:12-15).

In these words Paul makes two general observations about conditions. He says first, ". . . all that will live godly in Christ Jesus shall suffer persecution." Now "living godly" apparently implies that these believers will be living openly, honestly, in their testimony that they believe in God and want to walk in the will of God. They will be doing the things that God wants them to do. To live godly refers to the outward appearance of a person's conduct, such as being reverent toward God, respectful toward those in authority, considerate about other people, and kind to the poor. That is like God. To live godly in Christ

Jesus means that these people lived in this fashion through the grace that they received from Jesus Christ. Paul was conscious that no person in himself can meet these standards and have these attitudes; man needs the grace of God shown to him, given to him, through the living Lord Jesus Christ. And so Paul makes this comment, "All that will live godly in Christ Jesus shall suffer persecution."

"But evil men and seducers shall wax worse and worse, deceiving, and being deceived." Paul gives Timothy no instruction to confront these. He does not tell Timothy how to instruct them. He does not tell Timothy to argue with them. He does not tell Timothy to point out where they were wrong, to contend with them, or to get in any conflict with them or spend himself in contradicting them. They will be around, but this is how Paul admonishes Timothy: "But continue thou in the things which thou hast learned and hast been assured of, knowing of whom thou hast learned them."

How does anybody learn the things of God? God is invisible. A person learns the things of God by hearing people talking about them, by hearing other persons explaining them. I should ask myself, what do I talk about at home? What goes on at our dining room table? What are we discussing when our folks get together? The reason I should ask such questions is this: Would children learn the ways of God in my home? Perhaps children could get some idea of God if they watched my conduct. But this is not definite enough. How does anyone actually learn the truth? It is necessary to talk about it. I will have to somehow or other in my conversation bring out the fact that I believe in God.

"But continue thou in the things which thou hast learned and hast been assured of." How was Timothy ever assured of these things? I remember an old saying from my farm boy days, "The proof of the pudding is in the eating thereof." How can you be assured of anything? Not by what people say, but by what they do. And how was Timothy assured of the things of God? Not only because his mother and his grandmother talked about these things and told about these things and explained about these things, but also because they lived that way. Thus he was assured of these things.

Does it make any difference who talks about God? The

influence of parents is great. Scarcely anything is more impressive. It is amazing how many boys grow up with long indifference to spiritual things, and many times a blindness about spiritual things, and when you get right down to it, what do they go by? They say "My dad never talked about God." Those of us who work with young people are often saddened by the fact that one must lead that boy or girl away from what father and mother did in order to bring the young person to the things of God.

The influence of parents is great. It is persuasive also for good, not only for bad. In a home where the mother and father are members of the church and take part in it, it is most natural for their children to be in the church. Even when they are not in the church, they feel they ought to be. Even if they turn their back on the church and go out into the ways of the world, they feel all the time they ought to be in the church. Why? Because in their homes they had a dad and mother who were in the church. The influence of parents is great for good, and that is wonderful.

We come to the plain truth that "from a child thou hast known the holy scriptures, which are able to make thee wise unto salvation." What does this mean? Timothy heard the Scriptures, and they were explained to him. That was the kind of salvation that he could learn. To be wise means not merely to be informed, being wise means knowing how to act. What would a person do then? He would repent about self, he would accept the Lord Jesus Christ, he would believe in the Lord and he would receive the Holy Spirit. He would obey the Word. All these things would follow if a person were wise unto salvation through faith.

Chapter 15

THE INSPIRATION OF SCRIPTURE

Can you realize that the principle purpose of the Scriptures was not for giving information to the general public?

The promises of God to save all who believe in Christ are not known by man naturally, nor are they ever discovered in the natural world. Nobody on earth ever imagined the Gospel, and nobody ever said anything like the Gospel in the history of the whole world, except those who came to know Jesus Christ. The writer of the book of Hebrews does say, "God spake in times past unto the fathers by the prophets." Those prophets wrote down for future generations what they had been shown by God. About their writing Peter wrote,

> For the prophecy came not in old time by the will of man: but holy men of God spake as they were moved by the Holy Ghost (2 Peter 1:21).

This is a simple statement, but we should not miss its teaching. The prophecy came not in old time by the will of man. It was not because Isaiah knew so much that he wrote the prophecy. It was not because Ezekiel was so wise that he wrote the prophecy. Those holy men of God wrote as they were moved to write by the Holy Spirit.

In this letter the Apostle Paul is writing to Timothy about the latter days. He has told Timothy that there will be perilous times, and he warns Timothy about those times. The times that are coming will be very, very difficult and evil shall abound. Under such circumstances, living in a time of confusion and turmoil, Paul is admonishing Timothy to trust the Scripture as the source of the saving faith which he had.

Paul wrote a classic description of the significance of Scripture in his letter to Timothy. These are marvelous words:

All scripture is given by inspiration of God, and is profitable for doctrine, for reproof, for correction, for instruction in righteousness: that the man of God may be perfect, thoroughly furnished unto all good works (2 Tim. 3:16-17).

Many versions in the English language are published in these days, and you will find those words restated and grouped in various ways in days to come, but no new version will ever change the meaning. We should not miss it. "All scripture is given by inspiration of God."

In our day and time we have had some people put forward the idea that the inspiration comes in the men. They do not give God the credit. They say the Bible was written by inspired men: Peter was inspired, and Paul was inspired, and James was inspired. They can wax very eloquent about that. But the Bible does not do that. The Bible says, "All scripture is given by inspiration of God." I know God worked through those men, but you will recognize in that passage from Peter (1 Peter 1:10-12) that those men oftentimes wrote down what they did not even understand. When they tried to understand it, it was shown to them that they never would understand it. It was given to them to write the revelation down on behalf of generations which would come later. On one occasion when Daniel had a vision, and asked God to interpret it for him, the interpretation when it came was such that Daniel did not understand what it was (Dan. 12:8-9). It is not that Daniel was so inspired or Isaiah was so inspired or Paul was so inspired. It was the Scripture, their production, what they actually wrote down that was given by inspiration of God and "is profitable for doctrine, for reproof, for correction, for instruction in righteousness."

What do we mean when we say the Scriptures? We mean everything we have in the Old Testament and everything we have in the New Testament. There is one thing about the Old Testament that you and I hold in our hands: the best scholarship I know about has agreed that we have the very Scriptures which Jesus of Nazareth handled and read from. So far as the New Testament Scriptures are concerned, nobody knows when they were gathered, who gathered them, or why they are put together as they are. All we know is that the New Testament Scriptures as we have them have been used in 1900 years

The Inspiration of Scripture

everywhere to spread the Gospel. It has been proven by actual results that these are the Word of God. So when we say, "All scripture is given by inspiration of God," we mean both Old Testament and New Testament as we now have them. When we say Scripture is given by inspiration of God, let me make this comment. We do not mean they are the result of a logical argument, nor of a rational explanation, nor that it was a philosophical production. These Scriptures were given as spiritually revealed from God Himself.

Paul said that Scripture is profitable for doctrine. Any time you have a Sunday school teacher teaching children, that teacher is setting forth doctrine. She may tell it in stories; she may tell it in illustrations; she may take the children here, there, and elsewhere in their listening to her and the way in which she talks; but her doctrine is what she teaches. When we say that the Scriptures are given by inspiration of God and are profitable for doctrine, we mean that doctrines taken from the Bible are the truth. They are what will actually lead a person to God. Any teaching a person does should be according to the Scriptures.

Often I look with misgiving upon many of our Bible story books for children. I always look to see if they say it all. Did they leave anything out? Did they put anything else in? Very few writers are able, without leaving something out or adding something, to retell the narratives of Scripture in simple language in such a way that children can grasp them. Because Scripture has power, anything added to it dilutes it.

Then Paul wrote that the Scriptures are profitable for reproof. That means they are useful for checking up on a person. The teacher will compare Scripture passage with Scripture passage, because all Scripture is profitable for reproof. To double-check for the validity of any ideas that I have or you have, we go to the Bible to find out if our ideas are true. We do not go to other books, we do not go to church councils, we do not go to great preachers; we go to the Scriptures and there we can double-check for the validity of anything.

"For correction . . ." How can I know what I should be saying? I should study the Bible, and edit my ideas according to the Bible. "And for instruction." The Bible is where I can find material that is authorized, that should be told and that I am to tell. And why would it be so important for these things to be known and to be revealed? Paul wrote, ". . . that the man of God may be perfect." This word "perfect" means complete, well-rounded, so that he can have a full grasp of the Scripture, "thoroughly furnished unto all good works." "Thoroughly furnished" means "thoroughly equipped." Unless what I believe about God results in some conduct, in some activity, some work, some performance, it is just not true. That is all there is to it. My ministry is to achieve desired results, and it can do that. In other words, the Bible is the supreme equipment for the witness of the Lord, as it is the supreme material through which we have a revelation of His will.

Chapter 16

PAUL'S ADVICE TO TIMOTHY

Can you understand why Paul would urge Timothy, in view of the confusing conflicts in the public mind of his day, to preach the Bible?

> I charge thee therefore before God, and the Lord Jesus Christ, who shall judge the quick and the dead at his appearing and his kingdom; preach the word; be instant in season, out of season; reprove, rebuke, exhort with all long-suffering and doctrine. For the time will come when they will not endure sound doctrine; but after their own lusts shall they heap to themselves teachers, having itching ears; and they shall turn away their ears from the truth, and shall be turned unto fables (2 Tim. 4:1-4).

There are all kinds of ideas which receive public attention when it comes to matters of religion. Many, if not most of these, are wrong. I mean to say they are not the truth, and so they are misleading. Many of them are barren. You could hear them, you could think them, you could argue about them, you could repeat them, and be the same afterwards as you were before. Paul was thankful to God for Timothy's faith. Timothy really believed the Gospel. That young preacher knew the truth of Christ Jesus and believed it. In view of the times as they were, and they were becoming worse and worse, Paul gave advice to Timothy. He wrote as forcefully as he could. "I charge thee therefore before God, and the Lord Jesus Christ." Both he and Timothy understood that God was the Creator and the Judge, and that the Lord Jesus Christ is our Savior and Friend, who gave Himself to die for us. He spent Himself for us. He poured out His life's blood on Calvary's cross for us, and so Paul calls upon Timothy, "As you stand before God who made you and before Jesus Christ who saved you, I want you to be careful about this."

Paul calls to mind the one Person who will judge the quick and the dead. But when Paul speaks about Christ being the one Who would judge "the quick and the dead," he means to say that the Lord Jesus Christ will judge us while we are living, and He will judge us when we are dead. You could also say Christ will judge those who are living in Him and those who are dead in sin. God has appointed a day when He will judge the whole world by the righteousness of that man whom He hath ordained, namely Jesus Christ. This one Person Paul mentions is the Lord Jesus Christ, who will carry out the judging when He appears and sets up His Kingdom. Paul wants Timothy to keep this in mind and to act accordingly.

Paul has one simple message: Preach the Word. Paul has repeatedly, in various of his writings, used this term "the Word." No matter whether a reader agrees with him or not, there is no doubt that when Paul wrote "the Word," he meant the Word as set forth in the Scriptures and made powerful by the Holy Spirit.

Not only did he tell Timothy to preach the Word, but then Paul presented a classic admonition for any preacher. Any preacher could take these words and let them be his guidance for blessing. "Be instant in season, out of season." That means to be ready. Enter into every situation and be ready to preach the Scriptures and to tell what the Bible says. "Be instant in season, out of season; reprove, rebuke, exhort with all long-suffering and doctrine." Keep the call of God before the people.

Timothy knew what the doctrine was, and he was to preach it. Timothy knew how to understand the will of God, and he was to tell it. Timothy should endorse only what the Word of God says and tell only what the Word of God shows. Therefore, "reprove" the conduct of anybody, any preacher, any person who is out of line. Exhort those who are lagging behind. "With all long-suffering and doctrine," be kind about it, but persistent. The worshipers all want the blessing of God, and this would come only through Christ Jesus. Timothy knew that. So Paul calls on Timothy, "You know this to be true. Tell it to them over and over and over again."

What makes this admonition so important and so timely is that situations will sometimes be unfavorable to Gospel preaching. The world is not always ready to listen. Often in times of distress, such as financial distress when there is a general overall business depression, when people get uneasy about their ways of making a living, those are times when people will listen to preachers who tell them about the God Who changes not. Thus there will be times when conditions are favorable to the preaching of the Word of God. But there will be other times when people are successful, when they are rich and affluent, when everything is going well with them, when they are not having any troubles of any sort, when they feel self-confident and so sure of themselves that they tend to forget God. Paul would call on Timothy, "Preach it to them, tell it to them even then." Even if the times are unfavorable to Gospel preaching, or the times are favorable to others who are false teachers, whatever the circumstances may be, see to it that the people get to hear the truth of the Gospel.

Then in verses 3 and 4 Paul wrote something that is very sobering. "For the time will come when they will not endure sound doctrine." There will be times coming when people even in church circles, even among believers, do not want to hear anybody talking plainly, bluntly about God and the Lord Jesus Christ, and about heaven and hell, and about doing right and about doing wrong. "But after their own lusts"—that word "lusts" does not need to mean immoral (though it often does), but it can mean their own strong desires—"shall heap to themselves teachers, having itching ears." Some people want to hear about social things. They will go far and wide to listen to a man who has some new view about how to deal with poor people living in the city, or poor people who are sharecropping the land, or the folks who are working as laborers, or persons that do not want to go in the Army. Whatever the case may be, some people want to hear these things, because that is what concerns them. If the preacher wanted to talk to them about Christ, they would take that for granted. Everybody is supposed to know about that. If he wanted to tell them about how the Lord Jesus Christ died on Calvary's cross; that would be old stuff. How Christ arose from the dead is something to talk about at Easter time, but this they are interested in now is practical business. That is the way they would put it. Actually, in all this they are following their own desires. Such people would listen to anything that seemed to favor them and make their own position appear to be the right one. The tragedy is that when I listen only to what pleases me, I can easily be led away from the truth of the Gospel, and that happens over and over again. Paul wrote to Timothy that folks would be like that, but in spite of their being like that, "You do one thing for sure—preach the Word."

Chapter 17

THE CONFIDENCE OF A GOOD CONSCIENCE

Can you understand why a believer needs to be careful about what he hears and reads and thinks, so that he may remain true to the Gospel and the Lord?

The believer is surrounded by all manner of conflicting opinions. Some might think that when you once believe in the Lord Jesus Christ that would be enough. The fact is that believing in the Lord Jesus Christ is an exercise of your faith within your own self, and that, like any other function, can be worn out. You can get tired. You can become weak. You may be strong physically, but if you do not eat, you will soon be weak. You could have a clear mind about your work and about the things that you are doing, but if you never sleep and never rest, you will wear out. So far as the believer is concerned, that faith is something that needs to be kept.

Faith is not constant and it is not self-sustaining. You need to feed it. Friends influence your thinking, neighbors influence your thinking, fellow church members influence your thinking. In being careful to keep one's mind on the Lord, and to remember the truth about Him, it is sometimes necessary to differ with other people. One may have to be outspoken in one's testimony, and this of course can lead to aversion. People may not like it. It may lead to cool treatment or opposition, and eventually come out into affliction. The true witness must be ready and willing to face and to endure this.

> But watch thou in all things, endure afflictions, do the work of an evangelist, make full proof of thy ministry. For I am now ready to be offered, and the time of my departure is at hand. I have fought a good fight, I have finished my course, I have kept the faith: henceforth there is laid up for me a crown of righteousness, which the Lord, the righteous judge, shall give me at that

day: and not to me only, but unto all them also that love his appearing (2 Tim. 4:5-8).

Paul wrote to Timothy, "I appreciate the faith that you have. I thank God for the faith that you have. It is a marvelous thing that you have received it; now keep it and use it. Be careful about it. Watch all things so far as doctrine is concerned, what teaching you listen to, how you organize it in your mind, and how it appears in the attitudes that people maintain." A believer can get to the place where he is inclined to act in a certain way because practically everybody else acts that way: they believe in God, they believe in the Bible, they never read the Bible, and they never pray. Here the believer must be careful. When he goes along with them in believing in God, that is fine. When he believes in the Lord Jesus Christ, that is fine. But when they do not read the Bible, he must differ. When they do not pray, he must differ. He must not follow them in such practice. He must watch in all things in attitude and in practice.

The true witness must "endure afflictions." He may not have it so easy if he stands up for what Paul is talking about. But Paul told Timothy, "Do not compromise at all." People may say, "You go your way and I'll go my way. This is a free country. We can all do as we please." The witness may not want to say anything about their comments, but deep down in his heart he will know that it is not true. The sun is up in the heavens, and the only place it will ever be seen is up there. God is in glory, and the only way anyone will ever approach Him is there. The worshiper must come to God in worship. If a person preaches that there is one Word of God, the Scriptures; there is one Lord, the Lord Jesus Christ; there is one way to God, and that is by way of the cross of Calvary and the open grave of the Resurrection; then he will need to follow Paul's guidance to Timothy. If a person believes in the reality and the indwelling of the Holy Spirit, and he is going to follow the leading of the Holy Spirit, he must hold to Paul's advice. He will find some people will not like him. They will call him too narrow or too reactionary, whatever it may be. They may not give him opportunities to serve which he would like to have. But Paul would say, "Do not compromise at all. Face all such differences openly."

The Confidence of a Good Conscience 171

Paul does not hesitate to use himself as an example. "For I am now ready to be offered, and the time of my departure is at hand. I have fought a good fight, I have finished my course, I have kept the faith: henceforth there is laid up for me a crown of righteousness, which the Lord, the righteous judge, shall give me at that day: and not to me only, but unto all them also that love his appearing." Paul felt that his death by order of the court, if the Roman court should put him to death, would be as if he were a sacrifice, being offered to God. He wrote, "I am ready to go," as if some lamb being put upon the altar were to say, "I am ready." In Paul's case he knew what was happening, and he was ready to be offered.

Paul looked upon his death as an episode in his pilgrimage. When Paul was going forward to die, he did not think that was the end of everything. When Paul was expecting to be put to death, he did not think for one moment that would shut everything off. He was on the way home. It may be that you are actually thinking, from time to time, that there is something wrong with your body, and the time may be short for you. If you are a believer in the Lord Jesus Christ, you can look forward to the prospect of death as an episode. I mean by that, death is not the end. You are not running up against a blank wall. You are not going out into the dark. You are not going to fall off any cliff. You are going to move right into the very presence of God. When the Bible speaks of those who believe in the Lord Jesus Christ, it points out that when they die they are asleep in the arms of Jesus, "safe on His gentle breast." This is how it was with the Apostle Paul. "I am now ready to be offered. As far as I am concerned, the time of my departure is at hand. They may kill me. All right, in this case I am going on home."

"I have fought a good fight." That is the testimony of a good conscience. He had done his part. As his days had come he had served as well as he could, and his conscience was clear. "Henceforth there is laid up for me a crown of righteousness." He had not fought to advance himself nor to protect himself. He had contended to keep the Gospel clear and unmistakable, free from error. He had maintained his testimony clearly before all men. Paul believed in God; he trusted in God; and he practiced righteousness in living, which is reverence toward

God, respect toward those in authority, regard for other people, and charity to the poor. Paul's conscience was clear. He had lived his life this way. "Henceforth there is laid up for me a crown of righteousness, which the Lord, the righteous judge, shall give me at that day: and not to me only, but unto all them also that love his appearing." Do you know what to expect about the Lord? Are you ready for it?

Chapter 18

PAUL'S FELLOW WORKERS

Do you realize that not all of the professing believers remain faithful?

Paul always showed a strong personal interest in his fellow workers. Many times when we talk about the Apostle Paul, we think of someone who stands as a giant among men. In all probability he was physically a small man, because he said that people had a sense of contempt for his physical presence. But his testimony, his ministry, his significance in the New Testament, and his general testimony as an apostle, have all served to give us the impression of his being a great, strong witness for Christ. Yet as you read the New Testament you find that he was always surrounded by a group of fellow workers. You read of Paul and Barnabas, Paul and Timothy, Paul and Titus.

Paul had a strong attachment to his fellow ministers of the Gospel. No matter how settled his own thoughts were, Paul showed a close personal affection for those who were with him, and a certain dependence upon them. No matter how profound his thoughts were, he was very conscious of the individuals who served with him. He was humbly grateful for the help that he received. He showed a keen appreciation of loyalty among those who worked with him. In his letter to Timothy this was very noticeable.

> Do thy diligence to come shortly unto me: for Demas hath forsaken me, having loved this present world, and is departed unto Thessalonica; Crescens to Galatia, Titus unto Dalmatia. Only Luke is with me. Take Mark, and bring him with thee: for he is profitable to me for the ministry. And Tychicus have I sent to Ephesus. The cloak that I left at Troas with Carpus, when thou comest, bring with thee, and the books, but especially the parchments. Alexander the coppersmith did me much evil: the

Lord reward him according to his works: of whom be thou ware also; for he hath greatly withstood our words (2 Tim. 4:9-15).

Paul's mind went from one to another of those who had been associated with him. Writing to Timothy, he said, "Do thy diligence to come shortly unto me." Paul needed help. Paul was in a human body, and while his spirit had fellowship with his Lord, he himself as a person needed the kind of help that another human being could give him. It is not good for man to be alone. Paul was never alone. He had others with him. And he needed the kind of help that Timothy could give him, and he needed it now. Paul wrote, "By all means come over as quickly as you can." This was a polite way of saying, "Hurry up and come as soon as you can. I need you."

"For Demas hath forsaken me, having loved this present world." What a sad comment! I am pausing here for a moment, because you and I should be aware of the fact that not everybody is going to stay with us in the ministry and service of the Lord. I also want to take note that this was a matter of record. The Holy Spirit took note of this. God not only notes what I do, but why I do it. Not only was it true that the record says, "Demas hath forsaken me," but it explains why: "having loved this present world." In Colossians 4:14 Paul referred to Demas, and when he did it was without comment. In the passage in Colossians, Paul had mentioned a number of his fellow workers, and he had something good to say about every one of them until he mentioned this man. Strangely enough, there is nothing said about him. Paul simply mentions his name. It is possible that even then Demas was beginning to reveal his inward tendency, and Paul knew it. Demas could not follow Paul all the way. He loved this present world, this present age, and Paul was just too withdrawn from the world's interests to suit this man Demas.

Then Paul went on to mention the others that were there. Crescens went to Galatia, and Titus to Dalmatia. No remark is made about that. This did not indicate there was anything wrong about it. It may well have been that Paul sent them. "Only Luke is with me." Elsewhere Luke is referred to as the beloved physician. Paul seemed to serve in company with a number of fellow workers. It is probable that Paul felt having only one companion was strange. Maybe that is the significance of his saying, "Only Luke is with me." Then Paul wrote, "Take Mark, and bring him with thee: for he is profitable to me for the ministry." When he used that phrase "profitable to me" he meant very useful, very helpful. This is the same Mark that Paul once left behind. There was an occasion when Paul and Barnabas had sharp contention over Mark. Barnabas wanted to take Mark with him, and Paul did not agree, because Mark had turned back when the going got rough on a former missionary journey. Paul at that time did not have confidence in Mark. But apparently Mark could change his ways and Paul could change his mind. How wonderful! When I say, "Mark could change his ways," I realize that in a similar way so could you and I. Thank the Lord! And Paul could change his mind. Oh, would not that be wonderful if we could be that flexible in our thinking, that when circumstances change we can change, and when people change we can change. Mark was different than he had been, so of course Paul's attitude was different than it was.

"And Tychicus have I sent to Ephesus." Even in the personal need that Paul had, he sent this young man to Ephesus to minister to other people. Then comes this very touching reference to his cloak: "The cloak that I left at Troas with Carpus, when thou comest, bring with thee, and the books, but especially the parchments." This great apostle humbly requests items that he needs. Here he is in a prison cell, or living as he did in Rome sometimes in his own hired house, but living in isolation and in custody, and so he asks this man Timothy to bring along the overcoat and the books, but especially the parchments, which we recognize were likely Old Testament Scriptures.

Then Paul wrote this word, "Alexander the coppersmith did me much evil." Paul was realistic. While it was true that Paul could be gracious and openminded on every side, Paul was not stupid. When someone did him harm, Paul knew it. I am inclined to think Paul would not take that so much personally; it would mean to him the man was against the preaching of the Gospel. "The Lord reward him according to his works." There is no vindictiveness in this. Paul was following his own advice:

> Dearly beloved, avenge not yourselves, but rather give place unto wrath: for it is written, Vengeance is mine; I will repay, saith the Lord (Rom. 12:19).

This is the way Paul has of dismissing this man who opposed him and who hurt him. He does not cast it off as nothing; he does not treat it as though he had not been hurt; but he turns it over to the Lord, and then he can forget it. The Lord will take care of him. But then Paul went on to write "Of whom be thou ware also." That means "Beware of that man. Watch out for him. He is mean. He is hostile. Avoid him for your own good." Paul did not hesitate to warn others about him. "For he hath greatly withstood our words." That man had been in stiff opposition to the Gospel. When Paul gives this kind of advice, we should note there is no malice in such caution. It was really precaution. It was just the way he saw it from a practical, realistic point of view.

Chapter 19

PAUL'S DELIVERANCE IN THE ROMAN COURT

Can you understand that to be an effective witness of the Lord Jesus Christ, it is most helpful to have strong support?

The public as a whole may appreciate the benefits of the Gospel, but people, generally speaking, do not want to hear about personal commitment to God. They want all the blessings, but they do not want to walk with Him. Just now in our time it seems popular to talk about Jesus, but when you listen you can find that there is an aversion to using the name "Christ." It is common knowledge that Jesus Christ is at the center of all that is said and sung by the believers, but any mention of His being alive instantly causes aversion and withdrawal. Paul's experience in this connection can be taken as classic for us. What happened to him openly and prominently may happen to any one of us quietly and obscurely, by ourselves; but it can happen.

Because Paul had appealed to Caesar when he was charged with disturbing the peace, he was brought to trial in Rome before the emperor. He wrote something to Timothy which recorded his experience.

> At my first answer no man stood with me, but all men forsook me: I pray God that it may not be laid to their charge. Notwithstanding the Lord stood with me, and strengthened me; that by me the preaching might be fully known, and that all the Gentiles might hear: and I was delivered out of the mouth of the lion. And the Lord shall deliver me from every evil work, and will preserve me unto his heavenly kingdom: to whom be glory for ever and ever. Amen (2 Tim. 4:16-18).

Here was Paul's strong triumphant testimony: "Notwithstanding the Lord stood with me." We should notice how he wrote, "At my first answer no man stood with me, but all men forsook me." Does that make you wonder what Paul said? We do not know what question he was asked, and we do not have his answer written out for us, but we can be pretty sure of its thrust because we can read of other times when he was in court. He may well have affirmed that as he stood there in court he was standing in the presence of the living Lord.

Apparently he did not leave any doubt in anybody's mind about his own testimony. He was probably blunt about it and frank about it because he was always able to be that way. When he was standing before Felix the governor he said, "But this I confess unto thee, that after the way which they call heresy, so worship I the God of my fathers . . ." (Acts 24:14). Paul never left any doubt in anybody's mind about where he stood. In this case his answer was such that no person stayed by his side. Shall we think that Paul had no idea of how his testimony would sound? Shall we suppose for one moment that Paul was so naive that he did not know what would happen? Perhaps we could properly think he was not paying much attention to that. Paul knew what he had to say; he knew why he was in the world. Paul knew perfectly well that his time on earth was measured. He was here to do God's will, and that was all he wanted to do. So when he had the opportunity he opened his mouth and spoke. He did it in such a way that people knew what he meant; Jesus Christ was alive. He put it in such a fashion that all the other people who might have been standing with him dropped back and out of sight. They did not want anything to do with that man. Is it not likely that Paul knew quite well what might happen, and he answered as he did so that the Lord's name would be set before them? Was Paul unconcerned about this? Apparently he did notice it. He mentions it; not only does he mention that no man stood by his side, but he shows his spirit when he prays that they may be forgiven. "I pray God that it may not be laid to their charge." Believe me, when I drop back from standing with any believer, I am answerable. I need to face God about that. It may be that that man says something in a way I would not say it, and he may say it in a way that I think rather bold, he may push it out in front and precipitate a conflict that I might like to avoid; but if he takes his stand for the Lord Jesus Christ, it is given to me: I have my humble responsibility to step up there and stand beside him.

Now let us note that when no man stood with him, "Notwithstanding the Lord stood with me, and strengthened me." What a triumphant word! "That by me the preaching might be fully known." This is an interesting thing. I know the presence of the Lord standing with Paul was a comfort to Paul; but do you realize that is not really why the Lord stood there? Listen, "The Lord stood with me, and strengthened me; that by me the preaching might be fully known." The Lord would bless this man Paul before the eyes of the public that the whole scope of the Gospel might be presented before the people. He could have taken Paul home. He did not need to leave Paul here. Why was Paul down here at all? He was here to witness. Why was Paul talking at all? He was to tell the story. This is exactly why the Lord stood by him and strengthened him so that Paul could carry out his mission. "That by me the preaching might be fully known, and that all the Gentiles might hear."

Paul had evidently the advantage of the emperor's court to use as a rostrum or a pulpit. You have heard people talking about making a pulpit out of their circumstances. Well, Paul did. They brought him into court, brought him up before the emperor, charged him, and Paul leaned back and told the Gospel story right there in the presence of the emperor. He did it in such a way that everybody else ran away. But Paul stood there, and the Lord stood with him and blessed him. Paul says this, "I was delivered out of the mouth of the lion."

Frankly I do not know all that means. Does that mean that Paul is speaking figuratively and just saying that he was spared from further persecution? Or does it mean that he was actually in danger of being thrown to the lions, as the Roman court would occasionally authorize for a condemned prisoner? But Paul was spared the common fate of the condemned, and now he expresses his total confidence in the Lord.

That was just an example; but listen to Paul, "And the Lord shall deliver me from every evil work." Paul looked forward with complete confidence to his further ministry. There were folks who were going to be against him. There would be things that would be contrary to him, but he was persuaded that the Lord would deliver him out of every evil work, in spite of everything against him; he was confident that the Lord would deliver him in any situation.

Does that mean that Paul would never be sick? I do not think so. Does that mean that Paul would never die? I am sure that was not it. When he spoke about the Lord delivering him, he was not thinking about escaping the ordinary human problems that we have. He was thinking about the Lord delivering him as a witness, that the Lord would set him free to speak out and to make his testimony go far and wide. It was not only in these minor matters that Paul was confident the Lord would overrule, but in every incident, so that Paul's testimony would go far and wide.

"And will preserve me unto his heavenly kingdom." Paul looked all the way to the end. He did not know when the end would come. He did not know where the end would come. He knew it would come, and when it would come he would be with the Lord. When he speaks about being preserved unto His heavenly kingdom, that included Paul's eventual death and resurrection and glorification by Christ. The believer in Christ never ignores the fact that life will come to an end in this world; he knows that it is appointed unto man once to die. But his glorious confidence is that he is going through death into the very presence of the Lord. Death is not the exit alone for a believer. Death is also an entrance. It is an exit so far as this world is concerned, but an entrance so far as the presence of God is concerned. So Paul ends his testimony by saying, "To whom be glory for ever and ever." Paul had written so boldly, so confidently, just as he stood in court so openly and plainly bearing his witness, but not for his own glory: all praise and glory belong to the Lord.

Chapter 20

PERSONAL GREETING

Can you understand why it is so important that believers should promote their personal fellowship with other believers?

> Salute Prisca and Aquila, and the household of Onesiphorus. Erastus abode at Corinth: but Trophimus have I left at Miletus sick. Do thy diligence to come before winter. Eubulus greeteth thee, and Pudens, and Linus, and Claudia, and all the brethren. The Lord Jesus Christ be with thy spirit. Grace be with you. Amen (2 Tim. 4:19-22).

One universal characteristic of all human beings is stated early in Scripture: "It is not good that the man should be alone" (Gen. 2:18). This is readily seen as we study the affairs of man. It is very important also to know this for oneself. When one knows that this is true, it becomes the part of wisdom to cultivate fellowship with others. Paul shows in this letter to Timothy how much his association with other believers meant to him, and how he went about cultivating this.

"Salute Prisca and Aquila, and the household of Onesiphorus." When Paul said this, you will remember he was writing a letter to Timothy, and he had touched on profound things. He had of course referred to his relationship to almighty God, he had written to Timothy about the very high calling that Timothy has had, and he had given Timothy advice and instruction as to how to proceed in the great ministry to which he was called. Now as he was about to conclude this message, we find that he brought to Timothy's mind, "There are others, and I want you to remember me to them." The name of this first person we usually remember as Priscilla. It is the same name, but the shorter version, Prisca, as used here. Paul did not forget that he had at one time boarded with them while he was ministering. They were tentmakers, Paul was a tentmaker; and they lived together. Also these are the two who helped Apollos understand more of the Gospel. You will remember that when that eloquent young preacher was teaching, he knew only the truth that John the Baptist preached. Priscilla and Aquila heard him, took him to themselves, and showed him the way of God more perfectly, more completely (Acts 18:26).

"And the household of Onesiphorus." Sometimes I think that it is the strange providence of God that these names in the New Testament should sound so unusual to our tongues and ears. This is a man who had been a very faithful friend to Paul. Paul mentioned him earlier in this very epistle.

> The Lord give mercy unto the house of Onesiphorus; for he oft refreshed me, and was not ashamed of my chain: but, when he was in Rome, he sought me out very diligently, and found me. The Lord grant unto him that he may find mercy of the Lord in that day: and in how many things he ministered unto me at Ephesus, thou knowest very well (2 Tim. 1:16-18).

He must have been a great person to have as a friend. When Paul was in his most difficult situation, this man hunted him out so he could be with him, and help him. Paul never forgot it.

Personally I feel I would be smart if I would every now and again take time out to think on the past and remember the people who helped me. It is an easy thing to get the feeling that you are alone. But you should stop a minute, and think back. Have you had friends? Are there people living right now that have been friendly to you? Then remember them, and send them some greeting. Here was Paul, writing to Timothy, and though he was writing to Timothy, he was thinking about those other faithful co-workers that he had. This suggests something that would be very helpful for every one of us: keep in mind those other people. They will continue to be an encouragement to you.

"Erastus abode at Corinth: but Trophimus have I left at Miletus sick." Erastus was a companion of Timothy that we read about in the book of Acts, one of Paul's missionary company. Here Paul mentions that he stayed at the city of Corinth, very likely attending to affairs, doing things. Trophimus was at Miletus, but Paul left him there sick. This man was one of the company that Paul had with him. Paul used to go around with him. On one occasion when the Jewish people in Jerusalem accused Paul of bringing Gentiles into the temple, it was a rumor started by mistake. They had seen Paul associating with Trophimus on the street; and they assumed that Paul had taken him into the temple, which was not true.

Paul evidently placed his co-workers in strategic spots. When he left Erastus at Corinth, and Trophimus at Miletus, even though he was sick, you could just feel that Paul had been placing them around. By the way, let us note in passing, here is a worker, a companion of Paul's, and he is sick enough to be incapacitated. He is so sick he cannot work. Is this a lack of faith? Is it not true that some people would have you think that if you were everything you ought to be in the Lord, and had the kind of faith you ought to have, you would never be sick? Let us keep in mind that here is one of Paul's good friends and good workers who is incapacitated because he is ill.

"Do thy diligence to come before winter." Paul has his eye on the practical situation. You will remember he told them to bring his coat along. He had an eye on the circumstances, and he wrote to Timothy, "Consider what it is like. Look around you and see winter is coming. Act accordingly." It is no sign of a lack of spiritual willingness or appreciation of the power of God to be aware of practical circumstances. It is no sign that Paul was doubting that God would take care of him, when he made arrangements for winter. I know I am laboring the point, but some seem to believe that if you are a real believer in God, everything will be taken care of. It seems obvious you need to do some moving yourself. When there is a better time for anything, do it then. When there is a better way, do it that way.

"Eubulus greeteth thee, and Pudens, and Linus, and Claudia, and all the brethren." Here Paul named a number of his friends, his workers. Evidently Timothy was well-acquainted with them all and well-liked. He was that kind of man. Not one word of admonition or of warning about foolish behavior or unwise behavior about any one of those people.

"The Lord Jesus Christ be with thy spirit," the ultimate blessing. Here Paul was about to close the letter, and he was about to leave all with Timothy, and send him on his way. Paul had sketched out before Timothy things that he ought to do, and now Paul will end his letter. This prayer would be the final blessing from Paul, and Timothy could have asked no more. What more can one say, "The Lord be with thee"? Paul did not need to spell out what blessings would follow; the Lord would take care of Timothy. Paul did not have to detail what would happen; the Lord would provide and be with Timothy's spirit. Then came the closing words, "Grace be with you. Amen." Thus Paul ends this message to his beloved son, Timothy.

Titus

Chapter 1

THE ETERNAL GOSPEL

Have you realized that Paul feels it is the system of doctrine which promotes godly living?

There are many different ideas with reference to a human being and God, his Creator. Paul claimed that what made the Gospel of Jesus Christ unique and authentic was the fact that it affects the conduct, the personal activities, of the believer. This is a big difference. Paul claims that the Gospel of Jesus Christ is effective in transforming life, changing the ways of a person. If my way of living has not been changed I probably do not know the Gospel. The Gospel is not a matter of so many words, and it is not a matter of opinion. The Gospel has in it a certain call from God: "Come"; a certain instruction from God: "Abide"; and a certain command from God: "Go." Words in themselves are not the whole Gospel. The words give the direction and the response expected. That is what counts. Paul points this out when he writes to his fellow worker, Titus.

> Paul, a servant of God, and an apostle of Jesus Christ, according to the faith of God's elect, and the acknowledging of the truth which is after godliness; in hope of eternal life, which God, that cannot lie, promised before the world began; but hath in due times manifested his word through preaching, which is committed unto me according to the commandment of God our Saviour; to Titus, mine own son after the common faith: Grace, mercy, and peace, from God the Father and the Lord Jesus Christ our Saviour (Titus 1:1-4).

Let us look at this carefully. That word "servant" is much stronger in the original language. It really means a "bond slave," one who had committed himself to remain a slave forever. It was not unusual for a man to release his slave after the slave had worked a certain length of time, and had done faithful service. But it was also possible for the slave to ask the master to allow him to remain his slave forever. In that case, an awl was used to pierce the ear of the slave. This was a sign that he had foregone the chance to be free, and had committed himself to serve his master forever. That is why he was called a "bond slave."

Paul speaks of himself as the slave of God and an apostle of Jesus Christ. The word "apostle" meant a special messenger; someone sent with a message to deliver. "According to the faith of God's elect": that is, Paul was to stimulate and promote the faith of God's chosen ones. This word "elect" is also a meaningful one; but it must be carefully noted that it does not mean "select." To be in the "elect" does not mean that certain persons were chosen because they were in the upper ten percent of the class, nor does it mean that they were chosen in the sense that one was chosen out of three, or one was chosen out of five, or out of eight. The meaning of this word "elect" is that the person is called to come out of the natural into the spiritual. I am one of the "elect" when I have been called to come to God out of myself. I am to leave myself behind and commit myself into the Lord Jesus Christ. The word "call" is the basis of the word "elect," so one could say, "According to the faith of God's called ones, or God's chosen ones."

"And the acknowledging of the truth which is after godliness." This is the truth that is related to, and produces godly living in the hope of eternal life. That is the promise given in connection with faith in the Lord Jesus Christ. Paul wrote this as he did so that he might lead them on to accurate discernment and recognition of the truth which belongs to godliness.

As I was studying this I was impressed in a fresh way that the Gospel of the Lord Jesus Christ is actually designed to change my style of life. We remember how Jesus of Nazareth said:

> If any man will come after me, let him deny himself, and take up his cross, and follow me (Matt. 16:24).

Taking up the cross involves death; it involves crucifixion of self. Then what? Then the believer can live in the Lord.

This is a very practical truth: until I am through with me, I cannot actually live with God. I am to acknowledge myself as dead indeed in myself unto sin, that I might live unto God and the Lord Jesus Christ. And it will always be true. "Acknowl-

The Eternal Gospel

edging of the truth which is after godliness; in hope of eternal life, which God, that cannot lie, promised before the world began." Paul states again the fact that God had the Gospel in mind, even before He created the world and man. God knew before He started creation that this would involve His Son, who would come to die that He might save the creatures of God into eternal life. He was "the Lamb slain before the foundation of the world" and Paul emphasizes now that this Gospel had been known to God from the beginning.

"Which is committed unto me according to the commandment of God our Saviour." Paul understood that his mission was to tell the whole world, especially the Gentiles, about Christ. He then went on to give his usual greeting, "To Titus, mine own son after the common faith: Grace, mercy, and peace, from God the Father and the Lord Jesus Christ our Saviour." "Grace," the kindness and love of God toward man because of God's benevolent plan; "mercy," the compassion of God who "knoweth our frame and remembereth that we are but dust" because of our imperfect conduct:

> Like as a father pitieth his children, so the Lord pitieth them that fear him (Ps. 103:13).

"Peace," when all is under control and at rest because the goodwill of God is that the believer should be forgiven, be protected, and be assured. "From God the Father and the Lord Jesus Christ our Saviour": He gave Himself for us. So let us remember: the Gospel of the Lord Jesus Christ is designed to affect and to change our lives.

Chapter 2

LEADERS SHOULD BE GOOD EXAMPLES

How important is it for an elected officer in a congregation to maintain a worthy character and a good reputation?

Believers in Christ have fellowship with each other in congregations. It was never intended that a believer should be alone. He should be with others, and they should work together, pray together in service and in worship. Such a group needs leadership, and such leaders should naturally be worthy examples to those who follow. In accordance with the practice in the New Testament such leaders were chosen by the group, ordained and authorized to serve by the apostles.

Paul assigned Titus to act as a supervisor among the believers on the island of Crete. Paul was concerned that Titus should be wise about whom he would ordain as leaders. Paul gave Titus a description of the kind of men they should be. This serves to indicate the kind of character all leaders should manifest:

> For this cause left I thee in Crete, that thou shouldest set in order the things that are wanting, and ordain elders in every city, as I had appointed thee: if any be blameless, the husband of one wife, having faithful children not accused of riot or unruly. For a bishop must be blameless, as the steward of God; not selfwilled, not soon angry, not given to wine, no striker, not given to filthy lucre; but a lover of hospitality, a lover of good men, sober, just, holy, temperate; holding fast the faithful word as he hath been taught, that he may be able by sound doctrine both to exhort and to convince the gainsayers (Titus 1:5-9).

Leaders should demonstrate certain characteristics such as the spiritual experience of denying oneself, reckoning oneself to be dead, being raised from the dead by the grace of God, being born again by the grace and the Word of God, and being

Leaders Should Be Good Examples

indwelt by the Holy Spirit. The Holy Spirit will develop these attributes and manifest them in the believer.

"For this cause left I thee in Crete." Those who are already believers should exercise supervision over new converts. The people in Crete were new converts, and Titus was an experienced man. When a person comes to faith and thus becomes a member of the body of Christ, he still has things to learn. One can belong to the Lord Jesus Christ and yet not know how to walk in His ways.

The whole relationship with Christ has one attitude toward the flesh: control, even denial unto death; and one attitude toward the Lord: obedience, following Him. A group of new converts may not know what good things should be done, or how to grow. They need to be taught. The veteran leader knows what is to be done and what is to be shared. He knows what is lacking in the new believers. He can arrange to have it developed by teaching them. Leaders are chosen to stay close to the flock so they may guide the believers into the blessing of God.

"If any be blameless, the husband of one wife, having faithful children not accused of riot or unruly." The family life of a leader in the group should be above reproach, blameless. That is not saying that it must be sinless. But there should be no conscious carelessness or disobedience. If a man is careless, he is to be blamed; if a man disobeys when he knows better, he is to be blamed. A person is not to be blamed for his conduct when he does not know better or when he cannot do better. I do not think God will ever blame a blind man for not seeing, or a lame man for limping. But a person is to be blamed when he could do better, and does not.

"The husband of one wife" refers to his kind of family life. It is to be decent. Having faithful children, disciplined in themselves unto God, would be a tribute to the father in that family. Paul tells Titus that when he chooses a man to be a leader he should choose one whose home life is what it should be.

"For a bishop must be blameless." When the word "bishop" is used in the English translation the Greek word means "overseer." Sometimes it is translated by the word "shepherd." I do not think that the "bishop" referred to here was a special office specifically described and entered into in a special way as some denominations have in our time. I think rather it was a position of responsible leadership such as any mature believer might fill in any group of believers.

In our modern time, we know how some churches have priests, and some churches have bishops and pastors. In some churches there are deacons, and in others there are elders and superintendents. These are all positions of responsible leadership. Such a person should be blameless as the steward of God. The word "steward" means agent, and an agent of God should be above blame; not that he is to be sinless, because no man is without sin. But a man accepting this responsibility must understand that he may not do as he pleases: e.g., such a man could be angered, but not easily.

"Not given to wine." This does not necessarily require the leader to be a teetotaler, but it does require that he exercise control about all kinds of stimulants. "No striker" means he will not be violent. "And not given to filthy lucre." I believe this means that if a man has money he will not be addicted to it. The leader among believers will not be dominated by considerations of money.

"But a lover of hospitality" (friendly, ready to entertain in his home); "a lover of good men" (this man should be appreciative of virtue wherever it is found); "sober" means a serious-minded person; and "just" means a fair-minded person with equitable outlook. "Holy" means one hundred percent, genuine; and "temperate" means self-controlled. "Holding fast the faithful word as he hath been taught" means believing in the Bible as he has come to know it, "that he may be able by sound doctrine both to exhort and to convice the gainsayers." The leaders are to be living, walking demonstrations of what the Gospel is all about.

Chapter 3

FALSE LEADERS SHOULD BE SHARPLY REBUKED

Do you realize there are many wilful and unfruitful teachers of the Gospel who can lead sincere people astray?

The Gospel of Jesus Christ must be learned. Nobody is born with knowledge of the Gospel. Even when one accepts Christ as Savior and sincerely turns to God, there is much that person does not yet know that he needs to know. The young believer is ready to learn. He wants to know more. He is willing to learn from those who say they know, because we are all influenced by what people say about themselves. Because he is humble, the young believer is inclined to accept without question, like a child, whatever is said; but if the idea he picks up is wrong, being sincere and humble on his part does not make it right. Should the believer follow the wrong guidance he will go astray regardless of how humble or sincere he may be. The only way to help such young believers is for the experienced believers who know the Gospel to confront, to contradict, and to rebuke false leaders.

This may seem almost a declaration of war, and it is. Many do not fight the war, but the war is there; and if we do not fight it we shall be defeated. Paul told Titus plainly,

> For there are many unruly and vain talkers and deceivers, specially they of the circumcision (Titus 1:10).

You may say there should be more people witnessing for Christ, and that is true. But we need to keep in mind that many people who talk are not telling the truth. Many who are supposed to be ministering, are not really preaching the Gospel.

The task of preaching the Gospel is demanding. The preacher is trying to take the things of God and bring them to man; the things of eternity are to be expressed in terms of time.

It is difficult to talk about invisible things and make them real to folks living in this world. The task of preaching is complicated by the activity of false teachers, and there are many of them. In the time of Titus, persons who knew the Old Testament Scriptures contradicted what Paul was preaching.

It is surprising today how many preachers, ministers, church officers, and parents, have taken up the old line of tradition from their fathers. If you tell these people simply, "You can be saved through the Lord Jesus Christ," and tell them further just as simply that apart from the Lord Jesus Christ they will not be saved, it is surprising how many will say they don't need this, but have done what the church requires of them. Because of this they must be all right. It is not easy to tell such people they are wrong. Such were the people who contradicted Paul as an upstart. They ignored and repudiated him, flaunting their contempt because of his simple style and unassuming manner.

Paul says about them,

> Whose mouths must be stopped, who subvert whole houses, teaching things which they ought not, for filthy lucre's sake (Titus 1:11).

That is fighting language. Such teachers must be opposed. By argument? Perhaps. By contradicting them? Yes, even by confrontation. Such teachers can and do actually mislead whole families. They teach that which is wrong, and they do this because there is money to be made. This term "filthy lucre" I think means money made by unclean tactics, by acting in a way that is not right. Such money can be filthy.

> One of themselves, even a prophet of their own, said, The Cretians are always liars, evil beasts, slow bellies (Titus 1:12).

What an indictment this was! Is it possible that because men move in certain circles they develop some cultural flaws? Another translation reads, "Cretians are always liars, hurtful beasts, idle and lazy gluttons." Still another translation reads, "These men of Crete are all liars; they are like lazy animals, living only to satisfy their stomachs." Now notice what Paul says:

> This witness is true. Wherefore rebuke them sharply, that they may be sound in the faith (Titus 1:13).

Is there any hope for people living in a society like that,

False Leaders Should Be Sharply Rebuked

where it would be common to lie and to be selfish, looking out for oneself? Could any person get anywhere as a believer? Note what Paul advises.

> This witness is true. Wherefore rebuke them sharply, that they may be sound in the faith (Titus 1:13).

This seems to imply there is a way out of it all. But it will take sharp treatment.

What a sober responsibility for Titus or for any young minister! When a young minister is confronted by popular speakers who despise his simple Gospel message, he must stand up and declare them to be unfit, unreliable, wrong. We can expect one thing for sure: this kind of action on his part will surely lead to his persecution. That will be part of the penalty for telling the truth.

Chapter 4

EVIL CONDUCT IS MARK OF WRONG DOCTRINE

Do you realize that believers can avoid *becoming* evil, even though in themselves they are naturally evil?

Paul is writing to Titus to advise this young minister how to proceed toward an effectual ministry. The situation Titus faced was complicated by the presence of other teachers who were competing with the Gospel for the attention and confidence of the people. It is significant that when Paul deals with the limitations of false doctrines he does not discuss what is being said. That is notable. Nearly all argument we hear about religion is about what people say and what they think, and how they explain things. One person explains things one way, another person will explain the same thing a different way, and then they will argue over their explanations. Paul does none of that.

Paul draws attention to the way people act, contrasting the conduct of those who believe in God, and those who do not. Others are shown to be wrong not in what they say, but in how they act. What they say is also wrong, but Titus, instead of being urged to expose their error, is told to avoid it.

> Not giving heed to Jewish fables, and commandments of men, that turn from the truth. Unto the pure all things are pure: but unto them that are defiled and unbelieving is nothing pure; but even their mind and conscience is defiled. They profess that they know God; but in works they deny him, being abominable, and disobedient, and unto every good work reprobate (Titus 1:14-16).

That language, because it is Bible language, and rather carefully selected English language, could lead us right past the ugly truth to which Paul is referring. I am quite satisfied when Titus read these words he knew that Paul had in mind the

Evil Conduct Is Mark of Wrong Doctrine

very situation in which Titus was living. Let us notice how he says, "Not giving heed to Jewish fables." There were teachers who were talking, preaching, claiming to reveal the Word of God, not according to the Scripture, but according to what other people said. Paul urged Titus to guide his people away from this so that they would not give heed to Jewish folk tales, or to the commandments of men who turn from the truth.

When believers discuss the Gospel and non-believers enter the discussion, it is amazing how often persons who do not believe in God feel competent to judge God's actions. Paul urged Titus to warn his people about that. Paul then made a statement that is profound, "Unto the pure all things are pure." While wondering about that you may wonder who can be pure of heart. It will help to use the word "purified." The person who is purified is one who has yielded himself to God, has been forgiven his sins and has been born again so that he is a new creature in Christ Jesus. The spirit in him is the Holy Spirit.

Now when the Holy Spirit is in the heart and controls the heart, that person's outlook would be purified. The purified person sees the pure aspect of things around him. When a person's heart is right with God he looks for the right things. That would be natural. Of course, there are things that are wrong, but the purified person would not be interested in them. This does not mean that the purified heart esteems everything as being right, or that all the world is sweet and lovely. But in everything the purified heart meets and sees, the interest is in pure things, and the purified person moves in that direction.

"But unto them that are defiled and unbelieving is nothing pure." This is one sad thing about the human being: he can spoil and besmirch any clean thing when his own hands are dirty. He smears everything with his own filth. One interpreter expresses it thus, "For his dirty mind and rebellious heart color all he sees and hears." Paul wrote to the young preacher Titus, urging him to impress upon his people the importance of staying away from the mud holes. Paul then wrote in a more positive way: "They profess that they know God; but in works they deny him." Such persons claim they know God but their actions deny it. "Being abominable, and disobedient, and unto every good work reprobate." They are rotten and disobedient, worthless so far as doing anything good is concerned.

    This is a sweeping indictment which Paul makes about those who preach and teach ideas other than the Gospel. It is actually an application of this statement of the Lord Himself, "By their fruits you shall know them." The real criterion for judging soundness is not so much in what the person says as it is in what the person does. And throughout this book Paul is consistently urging Titus to note that it is godliness which certifies the true Gospel. This is at once an illuminating and a sobering thought, but it is salutary; it is good for me to know it. I should turn my face toward the light and walk that way.

Chapter 5

ADMONITIONS TO THE MATURE

Can you understand why Paul wrote about conduct when he was advising Titus about sound doctrine?

In his letter to Titus, Paul emphasizes that the distinguishing character of the Gospel is that it results in godliness. We shall see that Paul described sound doctrine, not so much that it is true, or that it is accurate or historical or Biblical, but that it is sound. We shall see that to be sound this teaching must produce godliness in living.

> But speak thou the things which become sound doctrine: that the aged men be sober, grave, temperate, sound in faith, in charity, in patience (Titus 2:1-2).

We count on the Holy Spirit producing His fruits in the believer by the grace of God. This is the basis of our confidence. We may well ask what part the preacher has. Why should the preacher (in this case Titus) speak the things which become sound doctrine? Isn't the individual believer going to have it happen to him by the grace of God? And the fact that the preacher will talk about these matters, does this mean such godliness is going to be the result of personal effort? That is not what the Gospel teaches. The truth is that the Holy Spirit will prompt the believer to do all things pleasing to the Father.

This Holy Spirit within moves me to want to do all things pleasing to the Father. He who preaches is co-worker with the Holy Spirit—the preacher defines the situation in which I can be pleasing to the Father. Now the preacher cannot affect my disposition to want to do it; this is the work of the Holy Spirit of God.

Another translation of verse 2 reads like this, "Be temperate, venerable (serious), sensible, self-controlled; sound in the faith, in the love, and in the steadfastness and patience." While still another translation reads, "Teach the older men to be serious and unruffled; they must be sensible, knowing and believing the truth and doing everything with love and patience." Their attitude toward self is that they will deny their own intentions and wishes, and will control themselves; but toward God they will be reverent; toward others they will be considerate; and toward life as a whole they will be consistent.

> The aged women likewise, that they be in behaviour as becometh holiness, not false accusers, not given to much wine, teachers of good things (Titus 2:3).

Someone has translated that to say, "Bid the older women similarly to be reverent and devout in their deportment, as becomes those engaged in sacred service, not slanderers or slaves to drink. They are to give good counsel and be teachers of what is right and noble." As was the case with aged men, this admonition encourages self-denial, humility, reverence toward God, consideration of others, charity to the poor. While we have been noticing what is said about older men and women, we must recognize this is true for everybody. Those who believe in the Lord Jesus Christ will find this guidance appropriate. Older men and women are not being singled out.

Older women are further spoken to:

> That they may teach the young women to be sober, to love their husbands, to love their children, to be discreet, chaste, keepers at home, good, obedient to their own husbands, that the word of God be not blasphemed (Titus 2:4-5).

All of these characteristics will show up in the person who is humble, yielded, and committed to the Lord.

The apostle is concerned about the witness of believers to people on the outside who look at them to see if Christ is real. And the Gospel will be real if the believers conduct themselves according to Paul's instructions.

Chapter 6

ADMONITIONS TO THE YOUNG AND TO SERVANTS

Do you realize that the conduct of every professed believer matters in the spread of the Gospel?

The public generally expects the preacher to live in an exemplary manner; and members of the congregation expect their officers also to live in that manner. That is proper. However, today it is not usually expected that every church member should be godly, yet this is the plan of the Gospel. So far as the Bible is concerned, every person, young and old, men and women, all who name the name of the Lord Jesus Christ and claim to belong to Him, are expected to be indwelt by the Holy Spirit. He will move that person in the direction of love, joy, peace, long-suffering, goodness, gentleness, meekness, self-control and faith.

The preacher is expected to set the example for his people, but the members also should follow the preacher. To be sure, the preacher and the officers can be expected to pray to God, but every member in the church can also be expected to pray and seek communion with God. Paul is telling Titus, in his capacity as a supervisor of certain churches, how to lead the people. All kinds of ideas are being set forth, but Paul explains that the distinguishing characteristic of the Gospel of Christ will be changed lives. Believers will be different. The ungodly will become godly.

> Young men likewise exhort to be sober minded (Titus 2:6).

It has been popular to cast aspersions at long-faced Christians. I appreciate the fact that long-faced people are not very attractive, but they might be right. There could be situations in a community that should make any person long-faced, sober. I am inclined to say, as I have grown older, that if we are honest there are many times we cannot feel light-hearted. Another translation of this verse reads like this, "In a similar way urge the younger men to be self-restrained and to behave prudently—taking life seriously." This world has in it things that are hard to bear, and young men, as well as older people, should face this fact.

> In all things showing thyself a pattern of good works: in doctrine showing uncorruptness, gravity, sincerity, sound speech, that cannot be condemned; that he that is of the contrary part may be ashamed, having no evil thing to say of you (Titus 2:7-8).

The preacher teaches others, and Paul urges Titus to be careful how he does it. Here is another translation of these words: "And show your own self in all respects to be a pattern and a model of good deeds and works, teaching what is unadulterated, showing gravity—(that is,) having the strictest regard for truth and purity of motive, with dignity and seriousness. And let your instruction be sound and fit and wise and wholesome, vigorous and irrefutable and above censure, so that the opponent may be put to shame, finding nothing discrediting or evil to say about us." While yet another translates this passage thus, "Show yourself in all respects a model of good deeds, and in your teaching show integrity, gravity, and sound speech that cannot be censured, so that an opponent may be put to shame, having nothing evil to say of us."

> Exhort servants to be obedient unto their own masters, and to please them well in all things; not answering again; not purloining, but showing all good fidelity; that they may adorn the doctrine of God our Saviour in all things (Titus 2:9-10).

Another translation may bring out some of the meaning even more clearly: "(Tell) bond servants to be submissive to their masters, to be pleasing and give satisfaction in every way. (Warn them) not to talk back or contradict, nor to steal by taking things of small value, but to prove themselves truly loyal and entirely reliable and faithful throughout, so that in everything they may be an ornament and do credit to the teaching (which is from and about) God our Savior." Again another translation says: "Bid slaves to be submissive to their masters and to give satisfaction in every respect; they are not to be refractory, nor to pilfer, but to show entire and true fidelity, so that in everything they may adorn the doctrine of God our Savior."

We have been noticing how Paul was anxious that believers should demonstrate in their conduct what it was they really believed about Jesus Christ.

Chapter 7

THE FUNCTION OF GRACE

Did you know the grace of God has been given to affect the life of the believer in this world?

It is commonly understood among people who hear the Gospel that the grace of God is involved in the forgiveness of sins. Now we shall see that Paul emphasizes to Titus that the grace of God is given for living in this world, also. It is wonderfully true that by the grace of God we are forgiven, but it is also true that by the grace of God we are empowered. It is true that by the power of God we have been born again through believing in Him, but the born-again person needs strength, and that strength does not come from his physical food. What Paul calls the grace of God is given to us by the Scriptures we read and the Holy Spirit working in us. This is the one thing that has the promise of enabling us to appear acceptable in His sight.

Not only is it gloriously true that by the grace of God the believer is reconciled to God, kept in His love, and eventually brought into His presence by His power and by His grace; but the believer is also enabled by the grace of God to live a godly life.

> For the grace of God that bringeth salvation hath appeared to all men. Teaching us that, denying ungodliness and worldly lusts, we should live soberly, righteously, and godly, in this present world; looking for that blessed hope, and the glorious appearing of the great God and our Saviour Jesus Christ; who gave himself for us, that he might redeem us from all iniquity, and purify unto himself a peculiar people, zealous of good works (Titus 2:11-14).

This marvelous passage bears careful scrutiny. "For the grace of God that bringeth salvation" is a statement that brings salvation right here where we are in this world, among the people we know. Paul went on to write, ". . . hath appeared

The Function of Grace

to all men," even as it was seen in Jesus of Nazareth. While all men do not have what He brought, yet He brought it for them. All men could see it in the incarnation of Jesus, manifested in the cross of Calvary.

Now this grace of God is actually "teaching us that, denying ungodliness and worldly lusts . . ." we have this precious gift and we can rejoice in it. But we have to live day in and day out, and sometimes our feet drag on the ground. We cannot trust ourselves to be always faithful or steadfast. We can summon courage to the best of our ability, and yet fail. How marvelous that something was given to help us. That was the grace of God, teaching by instruction and by example in the person of the Lord Jesus Christ and in other godly men and women who are mentioned in the Bible, that denying ungodliness and worldly lusts "we should live soberly, righteously, and godly, in this present world."

There may be some people who are trained so well in their childhood experiences that they live good lives. Still they could miss something here because they might think they live good lives through their own strength. However, in spite of their best efforts, they could fail. The grace of God enables us, as Jesus of Nazareth demonstrated. It was not always easy for Him. Do you remember the Scripture that reads, "My soul is exceeding troubled nigh unto death?" If that could happen to Jesus of Nazareth, should I complain if sometimes my soul is burdened? Paul said, "I have great heaviness and continual sorrow in my heart for my kinsmen." To deny ourselves the luxury of our own wishes is not always easy, but grace prompts us and empowers us to do so.

> Looking unto Jesus the author and finisher of our faith; who for the joy that was set before him endured the cross, despising the shame, and is set down at the right hand of the throne of God (Heb. 12:2).
>
> Looking for that blessed hope, and the glorious appearing of the great God and our Saviour Jesus Christ (Titus 2:13).

This points to the procedure by which believers can be strengthened. Just as Jesus of Nazareth gained strength by looking at the joy ahead of Him, so may believers be strengthened to endure self-denial by looking unto Jesus, "Who gave himself for us, that he might redeem us from all iniquity."

Early in my own experience, if asked why Christ Jesus died for me, in all likelihood I would have replied, "To keep me from going to hell." But later in my life I have realized that one reason Christ Jesus died for us was to "redeem us from all iniquity, and to purify unto Himself a peculiar people, zealous of good works," anxious to do the right thing. This is the work of grace in our hearts.

> These things speak, and exhort, and rebuke with all authority (Titus 2:15).

We remember how Paul said to Timothy, "Let no man despise thee." What we have been discussing is extremely important: we should make sure that we understand it. We can yield ourselves to God, and God will by His grace, His kindness, and undeserved mercy, actually lift us and enable us to walk well pleasing in His sight. We thank Him for it.

Chapter 8

PAUL WAS AN EXAMPLE

Do you have any idea what a person would look like who is eager to do good works?

The reputation of the people on the island of Crete was such that it would not encourage anyone to preach the Gospel there. They had been described by one of their own writers as "liars, evil beasts and slow bellies." Paul advised Titus in his preaching and teaching to emphasize certain things, reminding him that it was the will of God through Christ to purify unto Himself a peculiar people, zealous to do good works. Paul then outlined what these good works would be.

> Put them in mind to be subject to principalities and powers, to obey magistrates, to be ready to every good work, to speak evil of no man, to be no brawlers, but gentle, showing all meekness unto all men. For we ourselves also were sometimes foolish, disobedient, deceived, serving divers lusts and pleasures, living in malice and envy, hateful, and hating one another. But after that the kindness and love of God our Saviour toward man appeared, not by works of righteousness which we have done, but according to his mercy he saved us, by the washing of regeneration, and renewing of the Holy Ghost; which he shed on us abundantly through Jesus Christ our Saviour; that being justified by his grace, we should be made heirs according to the hope of eternal life (Titus 3:1-7).

Principalities are the civil authorities. Believers were to be subject to the local city council, or the governor, or the rulers of the nation in which they lived. "To obey magistrates," this meant that a believer eager to do good works would be a law-abiding citizen, even when the laws were made and enforced by the Romans, who were not believers. "Put them in mind," means that Titus was to tell the believers and keep it before them that they were to be law-abiding citizens. This should be the case even if in some cases the laws would bring hardship.

A believer who is zealous in good works will accommodate himself to the situation as it is. "To be ready to every good work" means to be ready to support and share in every good project in the community. "To speak evil of no man" would doubtless cut off much conversation. If a believer knew something about someone that was not good, he would never let it be heard from him. His business would be to show kindness and mercy. "To be no brawlers" meant that the believers were not to get into squabbles or arguments. The believer who is zealous of every good work indulges in no loud disagreement, but is gentle. It is important to keep in mind that it takes a far stronger man to be gentle than it does to be rough.

Paul says something about himself that sounds strange: "For we ourselves also were sometimes foolish, disobedient, deceived (about God), serving divers lusts and pleasures (about himself), living in malice and envy, hateful, and hating one another." This was an inward appraisal: this was Paul talking about himself. He was able to say in another passage that he had prospered in the Jews' religion beyond many of his equals. He stood in court before Agrippa and could say clearly that he had served God with a clear conscience from his forefathers. Here Paul gave an inward look; he lifted the curtain of his own heart. He did this that he might testify to the change that had been effected in him by Christ Jesus. "But after the kindness and love of God our Saviour toward man appeared," the love of God in giving His Son to die for us appeared in Jesus Christ, and this was what had changed Paul into the apostle he was.

"Not by works of righteousness which we have done." Paul knew it was not by any moral conduct on his part or his uprightness or goodness in behavior, not by anything he had done in himself: "but according to his mercy he saved us." This was Christ's purpose. "By the washing of regeneration" Paul had been born again, leaving the cocoon behind and stepping forth anew. "And renewing of the Holy Ghost." Paul had become a new creature in Christ Jesus: the new life that he had in the Lord was from and by the grace of God and by the power of God.

Chapter 9

BELIEVERS SHOULD MAINTAIN GOOD WORKS

Can you see how good works have the same relation to a believer that feathers have to a chicken?

Paul took pains to make it clear that the truth in Christ, which Titus was to be teaching and preaching, required honesty and diligence. It would eventually change conduct. Some years ago I was in a foreign country where it was a common characteristic of the culture for people to lie. When I told my wife about it, she did not even raise an eyebrow, but said, "So what is new about that?" It may be true that everybody lies, but in that country it was acceptable. The people told me it was a cultural trait, so that when anybody gave an account of anything, no one believed him. A person was not expected to tell the truth. Christian believers in that society told me that the only people who could be trusted were the Christians. They told me that truthfulness was carefully nurtured by the believers. If a church member were caught in a lie he would be warned, and if he lied twice he would be put out of the church fellowship. Church members were expected to be at every public worship service; if they were absent they were obliged to explain why. If any missed as many as two prayer meetings in succession, they would be taken off the church roll. This seemed strange in a country where personal habits were so loose, where nobody was expected to believe anybody. I was impressed that the believers stood for absolute honesty. And God blessed their witness among their neighbors.

Titus was dealing with people who had a cultural characteristic of being lazy. Their own people said they were liars. Paul emphasized that Titus should preach that honesty and diligence were required. This has special significance for us because today we live in a world which is in confusion and conflict. All around us is uncertainty. The public view seems to be that leaders cannot be trusted. There are many cases of the exposure of dishonesty and theft, which seem to be not due so much to indifference as to disillusionment. There is abroad even today amongst our people a hunger and thirst for truth. This gives believers an opportunity to witness to the grace of God.

> But after that the kindness and love of God our Saviour toward man appeared, not by works of righteousness which we have done, but according to his mercy he saved us, by the washing of regeneration, and renewing of the Holy Ghost; which he shed on us abundantly through Jesus Christ our Saviour; that being justified by his grace, we should be made heirs according to the hope of eternal life. This is a faithful saying, and these things I will that thou affirm constantly, that they which have believed in God might be careful to maintain good works. These things are good and profitable unto men. But avoid foolish questions, and genealogies, and contentions, and strivings about the law; for they are unprofitable and vain (Titus 3:4-9).

When Paul wrote about the coming of the Holy Spirit he said, "Which he (speaking of God) shed on us abundantly through Jesus Christ our Saviour." This is talk between believers. The Holy Spirit is God Himself who comes to dwell in the hearts of believers as from God through Jesus Christ our Savior. And He comes abundantly. What does that mean? Whatever my need, the Holy Spirit is given to supply it; whatever my weakness, the Holy Spirit is given to strengthen and carry me through. That does not mean I will always do everything that is right; I am afraid my feet are too heavy. But the Holy Spirit is working these things out to the glory of God.

The Holy Spirit comes from the Savior. God shed the Holy Spirit on us abundantly through Jesus Christ our "Savior"; Paul did not say Jesus Christ our "Lord." The Holy Spirit does not come because the Lord Jesus leads me; the Holy Spirit comes because the Lord Jesus saves me by overcoming the flesh in me. "That being justified by his grace, we should be made heirs according to the hope of eternal life." We could say, "being reinstated into the fellowship of God and into communion with Him" because in my sin I was alienated from Him. But the Lord Jesus Christ effected a reconciliation. He changed God's

Believers Should Maintain Good Works 211

attitude, as it were, toward me. He propitiated God and justified me in the sight of God by His grace that "we should be made heirs."

Eternal life has the confident expectation that the believer will become an heir of God, a joint heir with Christ, thus the outlook for the believer is to belong to the body of Christ, serving God and bearing fruit, being inwardly enabled and guided. Because this is true Paul could emphasize: "This is a faithful saying, and these things I will that thou affirm constantly, that they which have believed in God might be careful to maintain good works."

Even if a believer tries to do what he is prompted to do in the will of God, he will not have it in him. But the Lord is able, and if the believer has the Lord, He will enable the believer to do the things he should do. This needs to be said over and over. To act selfishly and carnally needs no stimulation. No one has to tell me how to act selfishly; I can do that of myself. But to act humbly and meekly, in a way that will be helpful to others, is not natural. It does not come easily, it needs to be promoted.

Paul concludes his message with a broad matter-of-fact admonition in the Lord. It was written in a negative form but it has a positive message, "Avoid foolish questions, and genealogies, and contentions, and strivings about the law." Titus was to keep out of foolish, vain arguments, for they are unprofitable. Getting into that kind of discussion does not help anybody.

Chapter 10

BELIEVERS ARE SPECIAL PERSONS

Do you realize there is a limit to the attention a pastor should give to wilful heresy?

We are often inclined to think that a pastor should never give up seeking to win those who are definitely committed to views that are contrary and different from his. While we are thinking about Titus as pastor we can be thinking about ourselves and turning it over in our own minds. Suppose there are those persons with whom you have dealings who are definitely committed to a view contrary to the Gospel. You try to win them, but they persist in their wilful objection. Should you keep on forever? Should a pastor constantly be burdened with this objector? It will probably come as a shock to realize that there should be a limit to the effort we make to win such objecting people.

The pastor, teacher, or parent who is presenting the Gospel is bringing a clear message of salvation through Jesus Christ. The person presenting the message is the one who evaluates the other as to the soundness of his or her doctrine. If I am conscience clear that I am declaring the Gospel of the Lord Jesus Christ I can be humble and gentle, but I must be firm with the person who teaches something that is wrong. In writing to the Galatians, Paul said, "If any man come to you and preach any other doctrine, let him be accursed." That may seem to be rough language. There are those who think Paul "blew his top," so to speak, but it was more a matter of being definite, positive. Listen, if this is food and that is poison, there need be no wavering: food will strengthen, poison will kill. One is for good and the other is for evil.

The same is true with reference to ideas that have to do with the Lord Jesus Christ. Some are true, some are false. There is no reason why a person who knows the Gospel should make any concession to the false ideas. As concerns people, that is different. You can always be concerned about the person. But we are talking about the testimony, and this seems to be the meaning of Paul's word when he writes:

> A man that is a heretic after the first and second admonition reject; knowing that he that is such is subverted, and sinneth, being condemned of himself (Titus 3:10-11).

The man who is a heretic and continues to present a wrong view that would lead people in the wrong direction, should, after the first and second admonition, be rejected. The basis for this judgment is, "knowing that he that is such is subverted, and sinneth, being condemned of himself." Remember, here is someone in the group who claims to stand where you stand and to believe in the Lord Jesus Christ. He shares in the fellowship of the congregation. This person will go about doing wrong, knowing right well what he is doing, "being condemned of himself," convicted of guilt and self-condemnation. We should be patient but not foolish in a case like this.

Unfortunately some people are going to turn away from God, in which event they will also turn away from you. To understand these matters it would be helpful if one could be brought up on a farm. There is an old saying, "You can lead a horse to water but you can't make him drink." A farm boy will tell you this is absolutely true. You could present the Gospel faithfully but the hearer could have his heart turned away. Mind you, I repeat: they may not know better; if they are ignorant God will be patient, kind, and merciful; and we can be patient, kind, and merciful. But if they claim to know and if they have had any contact with the Lord and then persist in wrong views, we should let them go. That is what Paul is saying. A human being can have his eyes wide open in broad daylight and not see the sun. It is very easy: all he needs to do is turn his back to the sun. Just as he can turn his back to the sun, he can turn his back to God.

In the succeeding verses we come to the end of Paul's letter, where he took time to attend to little details.

> When I shall send Artemas unto thee, or Tychicus, be diligent to come unto me to Nicopolis: for I have determined there to

winter. Bring Zenas the lawyer and Apollos on their journey diligently, that nothing be wanting unto them (Titus 3:12-13).

Here is a responsible man. He has the burden of all the churches upon him. He has been writing about very important matters and yet he suddenly switches to little details as he closes his letter. But then he underscores the primary thrust of the whole letter as he finishes:

> And let ours also learn to maintain good works for necessary uses, that they be not unfruitful. All that are with me salute thee. Greet them that love us in the faith. Grace be with you all. Amen (Titus 3:14-15).

Does the believer not expect God in His providence to give him everything? Does the believer who trusts in the Lord Jesus Christ have to make plans about taking care of himself? When, as a grown man, I became a believer in the Gospel, I started to study the Bible to find out what it really meant. I remember how puzzled I was by this statement:

> Behold the fowls of the air: for they sow not, neither do they reap, nor gather into barns; yet your heavenly Father feedeth them. Are ye not much better than they (Matt. 6:26)?

For years I by-passed that verse. I could not understand it. And after awhile, when I was teaching the Bible, I looked more closely at it. It had seemed to me that it was encouraging people not to do anything. Then I took myself to task. Did I think it meant that the robin would sit on a fence post and God would drop worms into his mouth? So it dawned on me: I had seen robins and other birds, but listen, the robin did not sit on the fence post and wait for God to drop worms into his mouth. He searched for them. As I continued my study it occurred to me the robin is confident that the worm is out there, and he keeps looking for it.

You and I would be well off if we could just put our trust in God and be confident that He has provided. But because He has provided for us does not mean that we do not have to work. Working is part of the business. Believers are to be intelligent, diligent, and provident. They are to take care of themselves and their people; they have no special favored route. They may expect gracious providence to give them a break every now and again, but by and large Paul endorsed what I have just stated when he said ". . . that if any would not work, neither should he eat" (2 Thess. 3:10).

And so we come to the end of this letter to Titus. "All that are with me salute thee." Friendly greeting is always proper. "Greet them that love us in the faith." Would that be selecting a certain group? No, it is recognizing a certain group. They selected themselves. They believed; this caused them to belong to this company. And Paul's all inclusive prayer when he deals with anybody is, "Grace be with you all."

Philemon

Chapter 1

PAUL THANKED GOD FOR PHILEMON

Can you understand why Paul would thank God for every memory of another believer?

Philemon was written by the Apostle Paul, and it is unique because it seems to be a letter from Paul to a layman. We believe that Philemon was not a minister or a preacher. Timothy was a minister of the Gospel; he worked with Paul. Titus was a minister who worked with Paul. But Philemon apparently did not exercise any public preaching activity, yet he did have a very real relationship with Paul.

This is a letter written by a former pastor to one of the persons in his congregation. We can learn many things here about it. This greeting of the Apostle Paul was not a greeting that he would extend to everybody. Bear in mind that the Gospel is for all men, although it is not true that all receive it. No one should complain that those who receive it enter into a different and better relationship with God than those who do not receive it.

The same is true with reference to the greetings here. The Apostle Paul gave this greeting to a personal friend. One could ask another question at this point: Is it proper for a preacher to have special friends? Would you object to that? Think about it. It does make a difference when people turn to God. It makes a difference when people obey God. If two or three persons obey God, they are much closer together than another group who do not obey God. We should think of this when we read this letter.

> Paul, a prisoner of Jesus Christ, and Timothy our brother, unto Philemon our dearly beloved, and fellow labourer, and to our beloved Apphia, and Archippus our fellow-soldier, and to the church in thy house: Grace to you, and peace, from God our Father and the Lord Jesus Christ (Philem. 1-3).

Would Paul not extend grace and peace to everybody? It is true everybody is not going to receive the grace of God or the peace of God. But it is offered. Almighty God is no respecter of persons. The grace of God is offered to "all" men, but not all men will receive it. And there is a difference between the person who receives it and the person who does not.

In these opening words different persons are individually identified, even Paul himself, "Paul, a prisoner of Jesus Christ." There were many things Paul could have said about himself, but here he wrote that he was in jail. He was preaching the Gospel, and he had faith in Jesus Christ, his Savior and his Lord. "And Timothy our brother." This expression of "brother" does not mean biological brother. They did not have the same father and mother. This implies spiritual brother. We gather from the way Paul is feeling when he writes, and from the context of his letters as he is thinking on these things, this means a spiritual relationship. It is not make-believe.

Both Paul and Timothy believed in Jesus Christ and each trusted in Him. Each had received blessing from God the Father, the Holy Spirit of God. This made Paul and Timothy brothers. In another place we find that Timothy is referred to by Paul as "my own son in the faith." There is a sense in which Timothy can be considered as a son of Paul because Paul's preaching brought Timothy into the relationship he had with Jesus Christ. But when he writes to Philemon he refers to Timothy as his brother. He is seeing the other man in Christ. "Unto Philemon our dearly beloved, and fellow labourer."

Would it seem to be proper to tell people that they are loved? No doubt this is popular in a casual way, but apart from that, would it be all right for you to tell another person that you love him or her? Would it be proper to tell that person that you really feel indebted to God for the privilege of being with that person? Paul wrote to Philemon and he called him "my dearly beloved." We make use of something like that when we begin our letters with "Dear Mr. Jones," but that expression is not quite as real as Paul's was here when he addressed Philemon.

"And fellow labourer." As previously mentioned, there is no evidence that Philemon was ever a preacher, but Paul counted him a fellow laborer. Philemon was a supporter, a helper. Something I have often wished I could adequately express is that those who support the Lord's work are actually helpers in it, and are counted as fellow laborers. "And to our beloved Apphia." Some translations say "our sister." She was evidently a woman, whose name was coupled with Philemon's name. Was she his wife? We do not know.

Paul referred to Archippus as his fellow soldier. He mentioned him in another Scripture, "And say to Archippus, Take heed to the ministry which thou hast received in the Lord, that thou fulfill it" (Col. 4:17). Stick to your job; complete it; get it done! Whatever Archippus was doing, Paul wanted him to do a good job of it. "And to the church in thy house." This will help us to understand that the word "church" refers to a fellowship of believers. It is not an organization of any sort that has certain officers and bylaws, and program.

"Grace be to you, and peace, from God our Father and the Lord Jesus Christ." May God be kind and merciful and benevolent to you, and give you inward strength to do His will. "Grace to you" can involve and imply a divine enablement from within. A believer could move in the will of God by the grace of God. "And peace (the result of God's goodness) from God our Father and the Lord Jesus Christ."

> I thank my God, making mention of thee always in my prayers, hearing of thy love and faith, which thou hast toward the Lord Jesus, and toward all saints (Philem. 4-5).

No doubt giving thanks is always needful, and perhaps one could say fairly that the giving of thanks is generally lacking. We do not do enough of it, and because of that we are hurt. Giving thanks for other believers is surely often omitted, and that is to our distress. We are so prone to take our faithful fellow believers, our faithful church members, generous, kind, friendly people, for granted. We should not do that. It always involves a loss of praise to God. Paul tells Philemon why he gives thanks for him. We might give thanks for a child's health or a friend's kindness to us, and this would be proper. But Paul thanked God for Philemon's love which he had heard about. Philemon had acted in such a way that people talked about it and Paul rejoiced in what he heard.

"Hereby perceive we the love of God, because he laid down his life for us . . ." (1 John 3:16). Love that is real can be seen in action. Paul thanked God for Philemon's love which others evidently knew and talked about; and for Philemon's faith, about which Paul had heard. How would anyone perceive my faith unless he saw me do something that I would have no earthly reason for doing? The only reason why I would do that is because I believe in God, as set forth in Jesus Christ. "Thy love and faith, which thou hast toward the Lord Jesus, and toward all saints." This does not imply that Paul treated fellow believers the same as everybody else. No. He treated them in a special way. Philemon also treated fellow believers in a special way. And Paul appreciated that very much.

Chapter 2

PHILEMON WAS HELPFUL TO OTHER BELIEVERS

Can you understand how the kind, generous actions of a believer make his witness for Christ much more effectual?

Jesus of Nazareth said to His disciples just before He was taken up into heaven, "Ye are my witnesses." That is the word of the Lord to all believers. In any given community the witnesses for Christ are the believers. Someone might say "The witnesses are the preachers." It is true, they should be. But if the Gospel is going to get far in any community the laymen will have to be active. Everybody who names the name counts. The world is in darkness because of sin, and the true light that brings salvation is in the Gospel of the Lord Jesus Christ.

This is the situation in actual events that makes us very sober. The only way the world will ever know of the Gospel of the Lord Jesus Christ is by hearing the testimony of witnesses who believe in the Lord Jesus Christ. Because this is true, right here is the place for tragedy. It is a common thing and recognized everywhere that actions speak louder than words. And this is true even though the principal form of the witness is in words.

Paul wrote to the Thessalonians, "Our gospel came not unto you in word only" (1 Thess. 1:5). As I think of that I have in mind, "in words, surely." For that is quite proper. That is the first form. But as Paul wrote: ". . . not unto you in word only, but also in power, and in the Holy Ghost, and in much assurance; as ye know what manner of men we were among you for your sake." And this accents the very truth we are noting. The "manner of men" the ministers are, the kind of person the preacher is, makes a big difference.

From this letter we judge that Philemon was a prominent witness for Christ. Again, I do not see any evidence here that this man was a preacher, and I do not know that he was in charge of a congregation. But he was an outstanding person, well known for his witness and for his faith in the Lord Jesus Christ. Paul rejoiced in the fellowship he had with Philemon, and he prayed that Philemon's conduct in generosity would increase the effectiveness of Philemon's testimony. Philemon could have far more lasting effect when he lived what he talked about.

> That the communication of thy faith may become effectual by the acknowledging of every good thing which is in you in Christ Jesus. For we have great joy and consolation in thy love, because the bowels of the saints are refreshed by thee, brother. Wherefore, though I might be much bold in Christ to enjoin thee that which is convenient, yet for love's sake I rather beseech thee, being such an one as Paul the aged, and now also a prisoner of Jesus Christ (Philem. 6-9).

Paul is laying the groundwork for a request he is going to make of Philemon. He indicates again that he was always praying for Philemon. In praying for Philemon he had in mind that Philemon should become effectual as a witness.

> I thank my God, making mention of thee always in my prayers, hearing of thy love and faith, which thou hast toward the Lord Jesus, and toward all saints; that the communication of thy faith may become effectual by the acknowledging of every good thing which is in you in Christ Jesus (Philem. 4-6).

The recognition of the results of obedience to Jesus Christ, the results in Philemon himself, would actually enforce his testimony. Philemon could tell people what Christ had done for him. His words would be far more meaningful because his actions supported his words.

In our study of Titus we noted how Paul stressed that good works actually validate, giving fuller reason for believing in the Gospel of Jesus Christ. And in this letter to Philemon, Paul accents the effect upon Philemon's personal testimony because of his good works. He goes on to say "That the communication of thy faith": This is a rather cumberson expression we seldom use, it probably refers to the testimony that was given by Philemon to others. How would Philemon communicate if he was not a preacher? He would live with folks and they would

Philemon Was Helpful to Other Believers

see him and hear him. They would discuss things with him, and he would talk about the faith he had in Jesus Christ. This would be the communication of his faith. This would be primarily by word, but would be enforced by his life style, similar to the way Paul had communicated to the Thessalonians.

> For our gospel came not unto you in word only, but also in power, and in the Holy Ghost, and in much assurance; as ye know what manner of men we were among you for your sake (1 Thess. 1:5).

In other words, the actual ministry even of Paul the Apostle was not in word only. His life backed it up. So here Paul said that Philemon's life actually would back up his witness and testimony. Paul implied that the testimony of Philemon would be far more effectual when others saw all the good things which were in him because he was in Christ.

This principle is of much importance to parents and to Sunday school teachers, as well as to pastors. The implication is that power in testimony is not so much in the words that are used, or in the sophistication of explanation: what makes the testimony powerful is the manner of life a man has. The manner in which the mother lives reenforces her witness with her child. This is very important because it is a floor on which teachers, parents, and many friends can walk.

Philemon seems to have been one who was renowned for his generosity. His personal conduct had been an inspiration and a refreshment to many.

> For we have great joy and consolation in thy love, because the bowels of the saints are refreshed by thee, brother (Philem. 7).

Today we would say "our hearts are warmed" when we talk about Philemon. We have not heard that he traveled with Paul, but in his own community he was, by his conduct, a source of inspiration to many people. Verses 8 and 9 seem to imply that Paul had been personally involved in Philemon's life in some such way that Paul could ask a favor for himself, with humility. Paul does not try to coerce Philemon because of any claim he may have. He gives Philemon an opportunity to act freely in love in this matter.

Paul was an old man, a minister of the Gospel of Jesus Christ, in prison because of that. Philemon could act on behalf of Paul for what he was. Rather than recall some previous situation in which Paul did something for Philemon, Paul presents himself as he is now—an old man, an ambassador for Jesus Christ, in prison for preaching the Gospel. He makes no attempt to change the circumstances. That is the situation in which Philemon could help him, and Paul wants him to do that.

Chapter 3

PHILEMON WAS ASKED TO RECEIVE ONESIMUS GRACIOUSLY

Can you understand how it is possible that a believer can actually treat a wrongdoer as if no wrong had been done?

The letter to Philemon is a plea on the part of Paul, one believer, to Philemon, another believer, who was known for his kindness and his generosity on behalf of other believers who were in need. Paul pleaded that Philemon should forgive a runaway slave and should now even receive him as a brother. The slave, Onesimus, had run away from Philemon. In the course of his wandering he had met Paul, in jail at the time; and they had become friends. Paul had won Onesimus to the Lord, and now sent him back to his master in order that he could fulfill his obligation as a slave.

Some have wondered about the ethics of this act on the part of Paul. Was it right for Paul to ask Philemon to take Onesimus back and treat him like a brother? Let me ask this question: When God forgives me for my sins is He condoning sin, or is He making a special case of me and saying in my case it is all right to sin? No! No! Such manifestation of grace emphasizes an important aspect of God's forgiveness of sins, something we sometimes overlook. God forgives my sins because my sins have been expiated. They have been paid for. Christ Jesus paid for my sins. God forgiving me is not God changing His mind about sin. There is no change in the law of God—"the soul that sinneth it shall die." But God has allowed another One to pay my bill, to suffer and endure the penalty I should have endured.

In this case, when Paul wrote to Philemon, if Onesimus was to be forgiven Philemon must assume the loss, because Philemon was the one who was hurt when Onesimus ran away. Paul could have requested that Philemon do this and excuse Onesimus, because Philemon owed Paul his very blessedness as a believer. But Paul would not approach Philemon on this basis as an obligation. He made it plain he wanted Philemon to do this for his own sake. Paul wanted Philemon to have this opportunity of acting with freewill because that would be how the Lord would lead him to act.

Let us consider how Christ Jesus came to save us as His own. He did it because He wanted to. If the Spirit of the Lord Jesus Christ was in the heart of Philemon, He would prompt Philemon to pardon Onesimus for running away. This would be what Christ would do and this would be what He would prompt Philemon to do. So Paul wanted Philemon to act for Christ's sake, and for that reason he would not push him.

> I beseech thee for my son Onesimus, whom I have begotten in my bonds: which in time past was to thee unprofitable, but now profitable to thee and to me (Philem. 10-11).

This is a play upon the word "profitable." The name "Onesimus" can be translated "profitable." The word actually means "useful." Paul made a play on words here in saying "he used to be useless to you, but he is useful now to me and to you."

> Whom I have sent again: thou therefore receive him, that is, mine own bowels (Philem. 12).

That expression, when it is translated into our contemporary language, implied Paul's own heart went with him when Onesimus went back to Philemon.

> Whom I would have retained with me, that in thy stead he might have ministered unto me in the bonds of the gospel (Philem. 13).

Paul would have been glad to keep Onesimus as a servant, so that he could do for Paul what Philemon would have done for him. Philemon had helped Paul before, and now Onesimus could serve in Philemon's place.

> But without thy mind would I do nothing; that thy benefit should not be as it were of necessity, but willingly (Philem. 14).

Paul knew that Philemon would do anything for him, but he would not presume upon Philemon without his consent. Paul did not want this to look as though he had pressured Philemon

Philemon Was Asked to Receive Onesimus Graciously

into doing it. He wanted this gracious act to be done willingly on Philemon's part.

> For perhaps he therefore departed for a season, that thou shouldest receive him for ever (Philem. 15).

Paul gave another reason for Philemon to think about this whole matter. How could Philemon be ready to adjust to the idea that this servant, who ran away and caused him a certain loss, should be received back without any punishment? Paul gave him various reasons and now he gives him another one, "Perhaps he therefore departed for a season" (maybe he ran away from you for the time being) "that thou shouldest receive him for ever." Paul pointed out that Onesimus came to where Paul was preaching the Gospel; there he found out about the Lord Jesus Christ. Now he was coming back to Philemon and he would be Philemon's brother forever. Maybe this was the reason in God's providence why this happened. Perhaps this was the very reason he was allowed to run away: that he might come to know Christ Jesus as His Savior and Lord. Onesimus may not have known what he was doing, but God knew.

> Not now as a servant, but above a servant, a brother beloved, specially to me, but how much more unto thee, both in the flesh, and in the Lord? (Philem. 16).

Philemon was asked to receive this slave back and treat him as a brother. Can we realize what a challenge this is for us? Paul made every effort to help Philemon to be willing to share in this plan. This is a remarkable story that God has set forth before us. Onesimus ran away from obligations; he was won to the Lord by Paul in prison, and was so changed he was willing to return to his master. Paul was eager that Philemon receive him graciously, as unto the Lord, and so he wrote this letter urging Philemon to do this very thing.

Chapter 4

PAUL ASKED PHILEMON FOR A PERSONAL FAVOR

Do you understand the wisdom in Paul offering to pay any debts that the runaway slave, Onesimus, may have incurred?

A peacemaker often fails because the persons who are quarreling have no confidence in him. As long as the arbitrator, the one trying to smooth things out, offers only his own opinion, either or both of the contestants will feel that his own opinion is equal to the arbitrator's opinion. But when the peacemaker offers personally to make up the difference between the two, to pay the difference, there is another impression. Paul wrote and told Philemon that he personally would pay the loss, whatever it was, between the two: if Onesimus owed Philemon anything or if he had taken something he was not supposed to take, Paul would make it good. This meant Philemon would have no further reason to contend with Onesimus. It also showed how much Paul cared, how serious he felt this matter was for both Philemon and Onesimus.

There should not be a long-standing quarrel between a master and a former slave. They were now both members of the body of Christ. Paul offering to pay the difference set an example Philemon could not overlook. Also, this offer on the part of Paul was consistent with the grace of Christ, of which Paul spoke.

> For ye know the grace of our Lord Jesus Christ, that, though he was rich, yet for your sakes he became poor, that ye through his poverty might be rich (2 Cor. 8:9).

For Paul to offer to pay the loss, whatever it was, in the interest of goodwill was consistent with the grace of Christ. Philemon himself had received the Holy Spirit of God, which would prompt him to appreciate this kind of action on the part of Paul.

All of this will become clearer as we read it the way it was written by Paul.

> If thou count me therefore a partner, receive him as myself (Philem. 1:17).

Paul is saying, "If I am really your friend, give Onesimus the same welcome you would give to me if I were the one coming."

> If he hath wronged thee, or oweth thee aught, put that on mine account; I Paul have written it with mine own hand, I will repay it. . . . (Philem. 18-19).

Some people may say this was just a gesture on his part, and it may never have amounted to more than that. Philemon may not have let him go through with it. But that gesture was in the right direction, and it was no doubt a sincere intention on the part of Paul. It may be well to note that all of this was going on between believers. Obviously this is not a policy that believers employ with all men. The application of this policy is to believers. When two persons believe in the Lord Jesus Christ and contention develops, a third party might enter the picture and restore peace. This happens among believers.

The application of this principle is not based on the persons. There is no discussion about Onesimus, nor is there any description of his circumstances. Nobody said he was in need. The whole focus of attention is upon the Lord: if Philemon wants to be well-pleasing in His sight, this is the way he would act. Treating Onesimus as a brother would not ignore the conditions under which they lived, but it would overcome any condition. If Onesimus, a slave, was to be counted as a brother of Philemon, who perhaps was a wealthy man, this does not mean that humanly speaking they were to be as brothers who live in the same house; they would not share all their property with each other. But there is a brotherly attitude on the part of each in the Lord.

> . . . Albeit I do not say to thee how thou owest unto me even thine own self besides (Philem. 19).

This was a rather subtle roundabout way of getting over this idea: "I am asking you to do this as unto a brother and if you feel you can do it, I will pay for it. I will make up any difference.

This is not to say anything of the fact that you owe me your very self." Or, it could have been expressed this way: "I will not mention how much you owe me. The fact is, you even owe me your very soul." Or again, Paul was implying: "I will say nothing of what you owe me, even your own self."

> Yea, brother, let me have joy of thee in the Lord: refresh my bowels in the Lord (Philem. 20).

This is Paul's way of saying, "Yes, brother, let me have some comfort from you in the Lord. After all, you have also become a believer through my ministry. Now let us cash in on that. Cheer and refresh my heart." Another way this could be said would be: "Yes, dear brother, give me the joy of this loving act on your part, and my weary heart will praise the Lord," or, "Yes, brother, I want some benefit from you in the Lord. Refresh my heart in Christ."

This is Paul's concluding and clinching argument. "Do this for my sake. Let me rejoice in this evidence of your obedience to Him." The argument by which Paul sought to encourage Philemon to take this action was not based on the need of Onesimus or his condition. It was a case of saying to Philemon, "It would enhance your image. You would have a better testimony. It would glorify the name of Christ if you did this. It would be a benefit to you, yourself, if you receive this slave and treat him as a brother. And you would refresh my heart."

Chapter 5

PAUL'S CONFIDENCE IN PHILEMON

Is there anything wrong with asking a willing person to do something?

It is not only quite proper to ask a willing person to act, but it is also very practical if you want to get something done. The willing person gets so much more done than anybody else because he is already set to go. If you ask a person who has not thought about a particular task to do it, he has to study, to think about it. But the willing person is ready. You ask him to do it, and he does it.

In this letter Paul is asking Philemon to do a big thing. It could only be done if Philemon were willing to sacrifice; to bear the brunt of the whole thing. Under the circumstances, the slave ran away and the master whom he left was the man who was suffering. And now Philemon is to overlook that. Paul felt able to say:

> Having confidence in thy obedience I wrote unto thee, knowing that thou wilt also do more than I say (Philem. 21).

How could Paul actually know this? He had past experience with Philemon. We get the impression Philemon became a believer under Paul's preaching. Paul knew what kind of man Philemon was. If we have dealings with a generous believer, one whom we know to be responsive to the call of the Gospel, we need not hesitate to go to him again with any need. He would probably count each opportunity to share by giving, to be a privilege. For those who do the asking, this can be a humbling experience. We come to a man and ask him to give something to a certain cause. It is not our cause and so it can be a rather touchy situation. Many people shrink from doing this. If a believer is actually seeking to promote a worthy cause, there may be some he would not approach, but there are others he would feel free to approach. And in this case Paul approached Philemon with his unusual request, but he approached Philemon with confidence. He expected that Philemon would do it, saying, ". . . knowing that thou wilt also do more than I say." How would he know that? He had had dealings with Philemon, and he knew Philemon was a generous man, moved by the Spirit of God to be generous with what he had.

This whole letter was definitely a request for practical support for another person; not for Paul personally. And the value of this Scripture in the New Testament is far more important than we would ordinarily think. Many times you may feel that the New Testament does not give guidance for approaching other people. We have exposition of our relationship with God in Christ, showing what we can believe, what we should avoid. All that has to do with what is between us and the Lord. Seldom do we have the feeling of guidance in relationships, between believer and believer. But here is a case where one believer asks another believer to do something that costs a great deal.

Some may say that if the Lord wants a man to do anything He will move him to do it, and nobody need talk to that man. That is one way to put it, and it could be true. But here we have the case where Paul writes to Philemon, suggesting to him what he should do. If the Lord would lead Philemon to do His will, is it possible that the Lord would use Paul to direct Philemon's action? Couldn't that be in the Lord?

I am more and more persuaded that, while I think there is much to be learned about this whole matter, I do feel that one believer can ask another believer to do something and this could be in the will of the Lord. Jesus of Nazareth told His disciples when they went out to preach in the villages in Judea that when they would come to a certain house, they should go into that house and expect to lodge there, according to the custom of the day. Lodging would be given to them in the will of the Lord.

Here we have a case where one man actually asked another man to do something about a third person; does this mean the first man took the place of the Lord? This need not be so; it may be that this is the form the Lord's guidance took.

> But withal prepare me also a lodging: for I trust that through your prayers I shall be given unto you (Philem. 22).

Paul has concluded this rather direct request in which he asks Philemon to do an unusual thing in receiving his runaway slave back home and pardoning him. He now ends by saying in effect, "I want you to get a room ready. I want to come and stay with you." Note the implication: Paul had just asked for a personal favor. Let us take this to heart. When dealing with another believer, if you ask a personal favor, you get it or you do not get it; but you do not cut off at that point. You have entered into his affairs, you have become close to him and asked something definitely for the Lord. You do not now break off; you will seek to develop that fellowship.

We find Paul practically inviting himself to stay with Philemon. In connection with that, he is also counting on prayer for God's guidance from Philemon and his friends.

> There salute thee Epaphras, my fellowprisoner in Christ Jesus; Marcus, Aristarchus, Demas, Lucas, my fellow-labourers (Philem. 23-24).

Here again Paul strikes a note of personal comradeship and fellowship. In writing to his fellow believers Paul has great regard for the communion. It is not good for a man to be alone, and Paul is eager to be with them.

Paul concludes his letter to Philemon with these well-known words:

> The grace of our Lord Jesus Christ be with your spirit. Amen (Philem. 25).

Paul's usual closing note is: "The kindness and goodness of God in Christ Jesus be with your spirit, be in you and strengthen you."

And so we conclude our study of this interesting and useful portion of Scripture, called the Epistle of Paul to Philemon, a personal letter written to a fellow believer in which Paul asks Philemon definitely to do something that would be costly for him. But Paul gives his reasons, asking Philemon to do this in the name of the Lord. And when a believer has the grace of God he will do what he is asked to do.